Never Forget Anything!

99 Amazing Tips to Make Evernote work for you

By Jay Castro

Copyright © 2015 by Jay Castro

Table of Contents

Preface

Dear Reader,

I wrote this book because I felt there was a need for a compendium of ways to use Evernote. Evernote is a great app and there are countless books on how to use it. However, there are not many references giving quick and easy tips for how to simplify your life with Evernote. This is what this book is all about.

This book was developed from my experience in using Evernote daily to simplify my life. I have included the all the ways that I know on how to use this app to make life easier.

This book is not a step by step manual or a how to book. The details on how to do certain tasks may change with every new version or platform. Rather this book is meant to impart ideas and get you thinking about ways to leverage Evernote.

This book is intended mostly as a reference so feel free to skip ahead and search for what you need. Then go back and peruse over the other tips and hopefully you will find new ways to use Evernote that you had not thought of.

Consider these tips as a starting point. The tips and ideas contained here should spark your imagination into new ways you can leverage Evernote to your advantage.

Best Regards,

Jay Castro

Introduction

Congratulations, you are now one step closer to making your life easier for yourself with the use of Evernote. As you may or may not have read in the books description, this book suggests and promotes the advantages that Evernote may provide for your daily life. It takes a look into what this free downloadable application can do in order to make your life easier with the use of the modern technology invented by the creators of Evernote.

Whether you may be aware of it or not, Evernote is your best friend when it comes to everything about your life. You may have heard of devices that may make your life easier, but the disadvantage is that it only will help you improve one or a few aspects of your life. Evernote will help you cover almost every aspect from when you travel to chores at home.

How does it do these fantastic things with your life? How does it make it easier?

Well, apart of its feature mentioned in the description about how easy it is to sync from one device to the other, it has many more. You will open your eyes to how simple it can be to organize your life within one simple application. From being able to write down all the items you need to do in your daily lives with the use of its built in feature to create to-do lists to keeping track of your coming up deadlines with the use of its reminders.

Be successful at home with Evernote by organizing what you need to buy at home, what needs to be cleaned or fixed and even staying on top of your home electrical devices by saving their warranties on Evernote, be successful at work when all your notes have been placed for your future research, be successful at school as you stay on top of your assignments and finish it before the deadline impressing your teachers.

This book does not just project how great Evernote may be for you, but it also provides for you to learn how to use this application to your advantage. Not just with paragraphs of constant information, but included with step-by-step guides on how to do what with this application and tips on the little secrets you may have never easily discovered about Evernote.

Imagine how productive you will be when you have an application that tells you what to do on what day, when it needs to be completed and a reminder before the deadline to be able to accomplish the tasks. With all this productivity, you will now have so much time during your day to more of what you love to do because of all the time you have used productively to complete those urgent and important tasks that is required of you.

Of course, more will be discussed on the following chapters. So, be sure to read the book thoroughly and become an Evernote master to master your life.

Chapter 1:
The Missing Evernote Manual

With Evernote, all your productivity and management needs are safe and sound. Due to its constant innovation and development, it is becoming one of the most used efficiency applications in the world today. The art of being organized should not be taken for granted, it takes a lot of forecasting and time management that even the most organized people have difficulty trying to adapt. The best part is, anyone can use it. Due to its simple mechanics and practical controls, you can be a professional architect or an amateur secretary and still have the ease and comfort of the application throughout your daily life.

This is the perfect tool to achieve goals in your personal and professional life. Most projects and everyday tasks are based on how we prepare ourselves for it. 90% of your efforts and successes are preparation, without it you won't know what things you need to accomplish or when you need it done. Evernote ensures that you get things done at the right time in the most structured way. Who wouldn't want that?

Basically, Evernote has a variety of ways to maintain your superb productivity level but here are the fundamentals:

- Take notes – you can't expect to have things planned out without your notes. Evernote's most basic advantage is its note taking capacity.

- Collect everything – Evernote assembles tangible and intangible sources, from your handwritten reminders to things found on the Internet. You can achieve almost anything with this combination

- Find what you need – Evernote makes everything easy to find again. If your life is simplified with sparse reminders and notes, you're living life wrong. You consist of various interests and events and this application makes everything accessible.

- Share your work – working on a group project? You can always share your work through Evernote without the hassle. This works great for sharing meeting notes, brainstormed ideas for your art squad, et cetera.

Don't worry it's free. Well, for beginners, all you do is make an account. Some features will be unpaid for so you can have a quick look around and get a hang of things. Having a premium account, however just escalates your productivity potential. Premium accounts welcome a more variety and specific actions and advantages.

One easy way to make sure that you can access all your Evernote account and details is by downloading the application to all your major devices. It doesn't take up a lot of space and if downloaded, is synced to all your devices. You should also download Evernote's handy partner: Evernote Web Clipper. You can screenshot and capture anything on the Internet and have it shared amongst your devices with the downloaded application. Topics that you can choose to screenshot would be emails, news articles and research for your personal and professional life.

You can use Evernote almost everywhere now and it makes productivity that more interesting. You won't need to worry whether your documents on your desktop has been saved on your smartphone when you're in a run, you can always just check it out on Evernote.

Take Notes and Save Everything

Note taking is one of the most essential purposes of Evernote (well, obviously originating from the name itself). Therefore, you can't get an Evernote guide without the topic on taking notes. You can store notes you will be able to refer back to in the future. Once you see the dire necessity of notes in all your transactions and day-to-day affairs, you will value the unique and functional note taking quality that Evernote projects.

Traditionally, you'll have to write notes manually on a piece of paper. Not anymore. With Evernote, there are just so many more options to choose from. It ultimately makes note taking simple and universal. That's a great factor considering the hectic-ness and diversity of tasks and daily happenings. Are you on the phone and need to write a number down? Save it in Evernote. Are you calling around to get a quote for a job or service? Right it down in Evernote. Are you brainstorming ideas for your project? Right those ideas down in Evernote. Etc.

What are the different note taking types?

1. Some people still prefer to manually write notes via pen and paper. Evernote takes that to account and has a partnership with your camera. You can just snap your notes and have it uploaded. As easy as ABC.

2. You can also opt to just type it directly to your gadget. Too lazy to type? Save it as an audio note.

3. It doesn't solely have to be a blank page, decide on having a checklist to eliminate things you have to do in a systematic way. Therefore you won't end up forgetting.

4. Organizing everything in a tabular form is even better. It isn't fitted to words on a blank page; you can create a table to simply store everything in.

5. Plus, you can write notes on your photos or PDFs to make it understandable. For example if you're working on a magazine, you can quickly comment on the page and directly point out the areas to improve.

6. You can create these notes into reminders so that you won't forget what you need to do, where you need to do, who do you need to do it with, why you need to do it and how can you go about it. Truthfully, reminders are blessings in an organized life.

To create notes, all you need to do is to pick a notebook that you want to add your note to. Click the button that will allow you to create a "New Note" and then it will automatically be saved on that specific notebook. Add a title, add some text and there you have it, a note in 3 simple steps.

The best thing about the notes is that you can always choose to edit some texts or delete it entirely. It is completely simple to do since it just requires you to open whatever note you want to edit and click any area that you want changing. That is basically it. You don't need to ask permission or click other buttons to edit something as straightforward as changing a spelling mistake, all you do is to click and edit. As for deleting the note, you can quickly tap the trash bin logo sitting on top of the note.

Collect Everything

The key to success with Evernote is to use it to collect everything. By everything I mean all pieces of information that come across your life, such as receipts, invoices, business cards, forms, reminder cards, insurance policies, etc.

There is no such thing as note type discrimination on Evernote. If you're confused, it really means that due to the various note forms that Evernote has adapted to keep, PDFs, JPEGs, Word form, et cetera, you can keep them all in one note. You don't have to have all the PDFs in one note and have your images in another. That's the beauty of Evernote's design; it prioritizes your substance rather than make you go through all the hassle to take down notes.

Here are some types of notes you can store:

1. Any type of photo format. There will be times where you need a photo or image to supplement or be the basis of your notes. By capturing shots or retrieving them from the Internet, it will be beneficial for you. You can also decide to just scan your documents or receipts. Who wouldn't want that? It makes you sleep better at night knowing your important documents and finances are secured.

2. Scanning business cards is also one of the astonishing but valuable traits that Evernote manifests. You use the camera setting and it basically scans business cards from blurry or terrible lighting to something comprehendible and clear. The best part is, it automatically examines the business card and stores all its information directly to Evernote, as well as partnering those information to their correct LinkedIn account. Perfect!

3. Did I mention that you could save your emails? Not in the format that makes the texts all jumbled up, but in an organized and practical way that reserves the emails in note form. Once you've created an Evernote account, you have an Evernote email associated with it. Send your emails through to your Evernote email and that's it, no conversion or adaptations.

4. You can even apply the web clipper feature that screenshots parts of sites that you want to use as reference. This is necessary when you're in the process of comparing something or collating different images. Imagine having a fashion inspiration through different styles

online, you just have to mix and match and your fashion line of work will soar to greater heights.

5. Tags make it an extra bit plain sailing when it comes to searching things on Evernote. These tags can either be specific to the note or can be shared amongst all the notes and notebooks. It's a faster and more comprehendible way of gathering information that is related to each other without having to copy and pasting them into different notebooks.

> **a.** To add the tags on your notes, open your notes and press the "click to add tags" field by the top part of the note. You can either choose to make a new tag or just use one that has already been created so it will be easier to connect them. For example, you can have two separate notes of your pet's daily nutrition and heart rates. You can tag the name of the vet that will look through these medical observances, prepared and organized for the next check up.

Find What You Need

What good is it to store everything in one place if you can't find it easily. With plenty of notes, images, documents and all that saved on your Evernote account, you don't have the mental capacity to remember where exactly you've placed them. Evertnote makes it easy to find everything.

Evernote allows you to search and forage for things under your notes and notebooks by pairing your search with keywords, tags, specific information on your business cards, texts, handwriting or even text that is associated with certain documents. How does this work?

> • There may be times where your notebooks are just filled with tons of notes. A notebook can be home to dozens and even hundreds of notes. It will just be difficult and a waste of time to search one title in a sea of records. The search box at the top of the screen permits you to find the necessary information in that notebook and if you want to have a more general search, you can always click the button with "everything" on it.

• Evernote labels almost everything. If you want to search for certain notebooks, you'll just have to search the title of the notebook under the "Find a notebook" field. This is mainly placed on top of your list of notebooks.

• As for your chats, you can always find certain chats with a person by searching their names or a general work or topic you've discussed. For example, if you have a work-related discussion regarding a festival, you can search the title of the festival and have a list of conversations in relation to.

• If you don't want to worry about constantly searching for a topic, you can always choose to save the search terms. This is great for topics that you will always use and look for.

• Furthermore, advanced searches make it even more straightforward. It gives a more specific search result. If you memorize the exact location where you have made the note or the date or perhaps the notebook, you can always search those words and information to make it an instant search.

• You can always have descriptive searches. What are descriptive searches? Above all, it allows you to search common words and phrases perhaps to find notes that associate them in. If you remember placing your vegan recipes in a specific restaurant, you can type "recipes vegan restaurant 2015" and it will specifically guide you to the note(s) you are looking for.

• If you don't remember searches you've just recently made, the search suggestions just pop up so that you can see a list of recent searches. It's great so you won't have to type everything out again.

• Although these are features only found in the Premium Evernote accounts, it isn't a nuisance to include that you can also search certain documents and PDF searches. Evernote is unique in the way that it can monitor and locate words and phrases written by your handwriting. Unless your handwriting may be scribbles and doodles, Evernote can detect and search it for you.

Share Your Work

Everything you create on Evernote can be shared. You can share notes and notebooks. You can also specify whether you want them to be able to edit your work or not. This is very useful when collaborating on projects. You can even chat via Evernote although I don't recommend it.

To share notes, first you need to find the note you want to send. By clicking on it, you have to press the share button and adjust the setting so the person or people you are sending it to will be able to solely edit the note, or simply view it without editions or they can have the power to edit the note as well as invite others to view it.

To share notebooks, you just follow the same procedure as the notes. Find the notebook you want to share and click it. Next, you will then need to press the Work Chat button and decide the amount of people you want to have access to in the notebook. Prior to clicking send, you can opt for them to just edit the notebook or edit and invite whomever.

You can share it; not only via the Internet, but you can share your notes in a group or meeting session by projecting your notes. You will be able to share your notes on a projection screen whilst pinpointing the things you're talking about and adding new things. This is a speedy way of discussing as you can go through the whole document in articulate detail and save it, ready to send it to the other members of the group. It is better to use this feature on a group-setting ready to be shared via Evernote or other methods. This will give you and your team the overall game plan and brainstorm that has the same notes as everyone else. If you want to look back at what has been discussed, it is available at Evernote.

How about having too many people editing a note? This is a problem for some because there is plenty of cases where one person edits part of a document and another person edits it back to its original form and the changes will constantly go back and forth. What Evernote has done is that it doesn't allow many people editing at once, you can see who has access to it at the current time and once they're done, the next person can proceed to changing it.

Tips And Resources

Still interested to know tips and tricks that Evernote has in store? Here are some more points that should be focused on. Some are points previously mentioned, but they have other beneficial aspects:

For taking notes:

• You can write notes on your notes. This note-ception concept makes it easy for you to shed light on areas of the documents, notes and images that you need to focus on. Note taking isn't only meant for texts, but now they involve images that are facile to understand and work on.

☐ Notes can also be used as reminders as ways to go about tasks. Almost, if not, all of your notes are related to time. You may have a note to write a letter to your subordinate or you need a note to remember to pick up your dog at the vet. It's all related to time and by having reminders to make the organization and management unchallenging; you will go about your day with ease.

☐ Checklists are just clumps of things you need to get done at a specific reminder or time. Grocery is the most popular one, but you can also have a checklist on what you need to do at a specific location.

For collecting everything:

• As I've mentioned earlier, you can send emails from your personal email to your Evernote email. There are a lot of people that love this feature since all those newsletters you have received; you can delegate the storing and segregating process to Evernote to handle. Other ways that this can be a huge help would be when you have your flight and booking details secured on your email, Evernote will transform them into reminders and notes so you can look back on them.

• Even when notebooks are meant to organize everything, you can place those notebooks to organize even more your things. For Evernote, there is no such as too much organization and it proves to be an advantageous factor. You can put all your notebooks that have something in common with each other and place them in stacks. In any way you see it, these stacks cannot be shared to anyone else and it is for your eyes only.

- For obtaining web page clippings, the possibilities are endless. You can add notes on them to show areas to improve on or you can directly edit them to suit your preferences. This can be shared with other people for the purpose of having group work done at a faster and more convenient way.

To find what you need:

- Shortcuts placed on Evernote will prepare you for searches on almost any note, notebook or work chat searches. With things going on, you don't need shortcuts for every note, otherwise... they won't end up as shortcuts. You may be focusing on a specific project or event, therefore shortcuts that are specific to that are necessarily highlighted. You can also undo or reverse those shortcuts in cases where you won't frequently use those notes as much.

  ☐ You can also opt to keep your searches at the ready by having saved searches. Just like with shortcuts, you can access the information that you have almost always been using so that it won't be a hassle in the future.

- You can sync almost anything from any device onto Evernote. At the navigation menu on your Evernote account, there is a sync button. By pressing that, you will be able to have complete access to documents that have been created on other devices. This leads to almost unlimited access without using a hard drive or other connectivity methods. All you need is to sync and it's done.

Sharing your work:

- With your shared work, you can see whoever is editing that document since it will have a profile and information on who exactly is on it. To prevent traffic on a particular note, Evernote won't allow a lot of people to work and edit on the same note.

- For a more comprehensive way of organizing and showcasing your work, you can opt to use the "Convert Line Dividers" layout so that you will be able to cut parts of your notes in various screen monitors.

It just expands your notes so you will be able to see an all-encompassing account.

• To combine working with other people on a project and the reminder aspect of Evernote, Evernote will provide notifications and reminders to your account if anyone has edited or included new information in your shared document. This will help you get anything done as soon as possible by constantly refreshing your memory on the documents you're working on.

Chapter 2:
Boost Your Productivity with these simple tips

Evernote has been growing in popularity through new developments of relevant productivity tools since its inception. Its purpose is to make our daily lives easier to manage and give the sense of all-inclusive reliability not found in many apps today. If you are fascinated to learn more, read the through the rest of this book thoroughly. To welcome you even more, here are a few tips to get quickly get you up to speed on Evernote.

1. Save your sanity and store your gazillion passwords.

A recent security article said that on average we have 19 user ids and passwords. According to that I'm above average and you might be too. So how do you keep sane? Evernote can help.

You have two options. You can store password hints or you can store the actual password safeguarded by a master password.

To store a plan text password key you would structure all your passwords by combining a master keyword with a master key number or another master keyword. For example, you could store My[Childhood Pet][Mom's birth year] and you immediately would know that your password is MyBlackie1956. The other way is to store the actual passwords in Evernote.

That's right; Evernote can automatically become the safe house of all safe houses. It's not to say that the passwords are shown completely out in the open, rather you can have the options to store those passwords in one main password. Although this may seem like there isn't any purpose to pursue the "password inception" (a password within a password), you can bet on it to be as reliable as anything. Would you rather memorize 10 different passwords and have your confidential notes out in the open? Me neither. Having one password that you can easily memorize will solve this dilemma.

How this works is that you select parts of a note and you right click it to reveal a list of options. Click the option entitled "Encrypt selected text".

Place a password in its place then viola. For you to come back to it in the future, all you need to do is place the password then everything will pop up as if nothing has happened.

2. Paranoid? How about securing your whole Evernote account?

You can have the option of securing your password individually, but you can also have the option of securing your entire Evernote account. Still skeptical? When you go through to your Evernote account, locate your "Security settings". Just by activating it, your account will then be coated with additional security.

3. Photograph everything and forget nothing

From business cards to photo memories to receipts, taking photos of everything will make it easier for you to remember certain documents without manually encoding it. Examples of this would be your passport, your drivers license, your prescriptions, business cards, etc.

4. Save typing and save voice memos instead

When you're in a rush and you just need to jot something down, sometimes typing it all down or scribbling an indecipherable language at the back of a tissue just won't do. Evernote is meant to be aiding productivity as well as keeping up with the fast paced lifestyle. To answer this query, the Evernote team has a created the voice memo option. If you're someone who uses their ideas and inspirations as their career of choice, such as artists or politicians, it is easy to make up a theory and concept then have it disappear once you're ready to have it written down.

Other uses of the voice memo could be if you're too lazy to type or if you are trying to save presentations in classes or record and interviewee for your article. There are plenty of reasons why Evernote's voice memo is an angelic feature.

5. Stop the email back and forth madness and share notes and notebooks instead

If you have a partner that you need to work a project with, you can just share your notes or notebook allowing you both the freedom to edit and add any information. Truly productive since you won't need to meet personally just to make minor edits.

6. Save your brain cycles for thinking and unload reminders to Evernote

Evernote needs to remind you about all the things you need to get done. Without this feature, people would have to depend on lists and scattered notes to determine what they need to do next. Often than not, it won't get done. Why? Because there's no trigger that would urge you to start an errand or project. These reminders are primarily the essence of productivity. There's no point in writing notes extensively of the things you need to do when in the end there's nothing reminding you to do them (unless you can recall everything single detail). The reminders don't have to be for a big event as what most people would assume. These quick reminders even for errands or tasks that would take a few minutes to complete would ultimately lead you to the end and larger result. All you need to do is enter a due date or time schedule then it will automatically alert you.

7. Favorites!

After fully indulging your lifestyle into Evernote, you'll have tons of notes and notebooks that you've collected. What better way to gather your most used tags, notes and all in one area that you can easily locate: the favorites bar!

8. To sync or not to sync, that is the question

If you have plenty of devices in your arson, you might not want to have every gadget storing the exact same information, especially when it comes to separating your work notes and personal notes. Another example where you might want to set apart your notes is if you're a lawyer and handling different cases mean segregating different information. Your primary case may be saved altogether on your Evernote in your laptop, whilst minor cases can be flicked through on your phone. You can do this by creating a Local Notebook. This way it stays in the original device and no one can open it anywhere despite having the same Evernote account.

9. Save time by saving your searches

Once you've become an expert in Evernote or if you've become an avid admirer of Evernote, you will realize that your tags, notes and notebooks have increased in size. It may look like you have hundreds of tags and searching them individually would be as close as searching Waldo in a sea of white and red stripes. You may opt for the search button, but if you're working on a single project, you can even improve your efficiency by saving those particular searches. For example, you created a notebook called "Project 1.23.14." with the numbers symbolizing the due date of the project, January 23, 2014. You can easily have the notebook on the ready without foraging through notebooks with similar and confusing titles.

10. Start unstructured and organize as you go

Don't fret about how you're going to organize the mounds of documents and information you have. Just start dumping everything in Evernote and tidy up as you go. You might find as you add more and more things that you can group things into notebooks.

You don't need to go through a long process to do it. All you need is to drag everything around to make it easier for you to sort out everything. Easy.

11. Free yourself from email madness and let Evernote track your to do emails.

Whenever you see an email that requires follow up or needs an action item, forward it to Evernote and inside Evernote add a reminder. Why is this better than outlook follow up flag? Because you can add comments and texts, you can add attachments, photos, etc.

11.b Unload the burden on your email and store reference emails in Evernote

Sending emails to your Evernote account may be something you need to do on a daily basis. For example your boss would send out memos or the minutes of the business meetings via email, you'll need to collate all these information in an app that would secure them and allow you to add additional information ready to be kept as notes or presentations. In other applications, you will need to forward each email individually into their productivity app. Although this is more specific and isn't prone to error, however it is time consuming. Forwarding more than one email is more efficient, even if you sent the wrong file, it can easily be undone.

Since Evernote has it's own email address, all you need to do is to send your email to that address. Your own Evernote email address is hidden in the settings of your Evernote account. What it does is that it will automatically file any email on a notebook. The title of the email will be the title of the note, the @ sign will delegate that note to a notebook. Don't forget that you can use the # sign as a tag for you.

12. Merge Notes to consolidate information

Notes can be easy to locate things, but with tons of them, you won't realize that you've created the exact same ones or realize that one is similar. Putting them together is the best option, by merging notes you can easily command your Evernote content. Use the Merge command from the menu.

13. Evernote Free or Evernote Premium?

Evernote is free for new users and will help those who are still new to the application, often exploring the different features it manifests. It doesn't give a wide variety of options but it gives you the assurance of ease and comfort. Premium, of course, is the better option for frequent users. Larger storage space, multi-device sync mechanism and transforming notes into immediate presentations, are just a few of the benefits.

14. Merge Tags

Tags are unlimited. However sometimes you'll end up with similar tags that should really be one. For example, Dad, dad and daddy should all be one tag. Home, house and myhouse should similarly be just one tag. The can be merged.

You can drag a tag to another one. If you don't remember where you've placed them, the tags themselves have an arrow pointing down. Click it and you can see all the other tags associated with that tag.

15. Images contain information too

One of Evernote's most powerful feature is that it can scan and index text inside images. Not only will you be able to tag images, but also you can include texts within the pictures. For example, you go window-shopping and find pieces that you just have to compare to other stores. Have your device at the ready and just take a photo of what catches your eye. Within the photo you might have jeans, a shirt and sneakers. When you search for photos with the word "jeans" on them, you can automatically link it tons of photos with jeans on them. Tag the shop they're located in and you're done.

16. Install Evernote Everywhere

Evernote can be used on any device; your only requirement is to download the application. Since it's free to download, you have no excuse for not getting it. Your Evernote account can open up documents made on your laptop, for instance, and can be opened on your phone. Bringing a memory stick or hard drive is so last year, keep everything online hassle free.

17. Keep some notes local

Unlike the previous the tip, you can always opt not to share some documents you've created on one device from sharing it to others. Sometimes, users would prefer to have their laptops filled with work related notes and documents, whilst leaving their phones free to upload and keep personal files. This is a wise idea considering the amount of information that you'll need to keep and the amount of tags are overwhelming.

18. Link with other applications?

It is one thing to link with other devices and it's another to link with applications. For your information, linking with other applications doesn't lose your content on Evernote; it just allows you to develop your productive means through other methods. Some people may not like the way Evernote scans the images or creates an inventory of some sorts, so you can opt for another app. Since it's linked with Evernote, you can just merge the notes together.

19. Use templates for common notes

Let's say, for instance, you have a blog that you need to consistently keep updated. Whether it is your job or whether you find solace in something that provides a medium to express your thoughts to a specific community, you will need to maintain the zest and interest by having updated information on those blogs. What better than have templates of blog posts that you can fill up on the go or when inspiration strikes? The blogging community has faced difficulties when writing down blog ideas since they just write it in notes and leave them to evaporate. Template formats would allow you to fill in bit-by-bit ideas of blogs that you appears all of a sudden. When you finally have the time to look through it, you can just write in additional information ready to post. Plus, you will be able to write plenty of blogs at once. By the end of the week, you'll realize that you have potential blog posts ready to be published and the rest of template blogs you can leave for future posts awaiting further developments. How do you do this?

All you need to do is to write a template of your choice as a note and then export the file. Once you need it in the future, it is ready to be used.

20. Clip websites

Ideal for taking screenshots of parts of sites that you'll want to use for future references. Plenty of wedding planners or event organizers absolutely adore this feature; it makes collaging bits and pieces of ideas from various sources and matching them up. It'll be easier to see the bigger picture with website clipping.

Chapter 3:
Leverage Evernote at Home

1. Save your Kids' Drawings and Doodles for posterity

Do you save every little drawing and every little doodle your little one brings home from Kindergarten? Most parents intend to save them but they get lost over the years. If you're not an organization freak then the next best thing is to capture everything in Evernote.

It's really simple. All you have to do is to gather all their drawings, scan them into Evernote and just tag them. This way you will have saved images of those doodles, whilst throwing away the physical papers. Just make sure you tag your notes for easy retrieval.

This saves plenty of storage space and you can even recycle those used papers. This is the perfect way to preserve the hundreds of doodles they make. It will be worthwhile in the future showing them timeless flashbacks of whom they once were. It acts like a time machine travelling back and reliving your children's history. They will thank you in the future.

Furthermore, it is a perfect reminder of the innocence of your kids once you're away from home. You will be able to bring copies of their creations; you will always feel at home no matter where you are in the world. Evernote is the perfect time capsules that will bring nothing but joyful nostalgia.

2. Trace your roots with Evernote

Tracing back your line of descent is not that easy to do. Considering the different levels and branches of your family tree, it is almost impossible to have a complete and detailed family lineage. You won't know if you were once related to a great marksman or perhaps, with intense focus and deep research, the inventor of the first documented hieroglyphic write in Ancient Egypt. By meticulously tracking down your relatives, your findings will amaze you. With Evernote, you can organize your notes, your documents and even your family tree.

How does it work? It's as simple as organizing your workspace. All you need to have equipped with you is your ability to organize every detail into its specific category. First, you will need to save pieces of information given to you. Be it PDF documents, voices, photos, et cetera. Save it in a name that you will remember this will be an easy access later on. With genealogy, you can organize each document given to you by placing the names of the people included in the said document. You will need to add tags in the note details.

The next step would be to allocate these notes into notebooks. It is a norm to have only a few notebooks. Once you place a note in one, it can't be shared to another. This proves troublesome when adding names from various family trees. What you can do is to make notebooks of completely separate family trees.

Finally, tags. Tags are useful in that you can have an infinite number of tags associated with one note. Evernote will allow you to link various notes in a specific tag. For example, if you are looking for a family member that lives in the Asia Pacific, you can research it in the tag and any family member related to the tag will pop up. Perfect for social gatherings, you won't have the hassle of asking them individually where they are.

Basically, Evernote is something you should consider when it comes to genealogy. It seems pretty bothersome at first, but with the correct use of your organizational skills, this will be breeze in the long run.

3. Save money by using a Grocery List

Have you ever gone to the grocery store to buy eggs and come out with a cart full of groceries?

Apart from the ability to save your children's drawings or creating a perfect wish list, either for yourself or for your friend, Evernote doesn't stop there. Evernote has the capability to provide for your entire checklist needs, especially when out to do grocery shopping.

The best thing about having a check list in your smart device is that: a) You carry your smart device almost everywhere you go, so gone are the days where you panic at the grocery store without your check list. b) It is stored with your other information, which can be easily accessed. Allowing yourself to see what you need 24/7.

When creating a checklist, you are simply asked to go onto your Evernote application, whether it is on your Mac, Windows, Android and others. Click the checkbox button that is displayed on the right hand side of the page. If ever you want to add more boxes onto your checklist, just click on the checkbox again and a new checkbox will appear for you to place what you need.

If you are on your Mac, then you can create your checklist by clicking Format, then Insert To-Do. However, if you are on your Windows PC, click Format, then To-Do and lastly Insert Checkbox or in computer terms CTRL + SHIFT + C.

Finding a hard time looking through all your checklists?

Well, if ever you want to look at all the checkboxes, which you haven't accomplished. Type in *todo:false* within your Evernote's search box, if you want to do the opposite and look for all the checkboxes you have completed, then type *todo:** into the search box.

One of the best features that Evernote provides is the ability to keep all your checklists in sync. One of the problems people usually face when creating a checklist is that their checklist on their smart phone, is completely different from your desktop or laptop. Evernote is able to sync both items, once you have logged into your Evernote. Basically, once you have checked one box in your phone, it automatically checks the box on your computer.

Pretty neat right?

4. Curb impulse buying by creating a Wish List

Whether you are creating a wish list for your birthday, Christmas or even a wish list for your friends, Evernote has gone above and beyond to provide for you a highly advanced system in order to create the wish list of your dreams.

Once you have registered for an account in Evernote and have downloaded the Evernote Web Clipper browser extension, wish listing will become a breeze. All you need to do is to simply right click on your

PC of the item that you wish to receive and add the URL, image or entire page onto Evernote.

Creating your wish list will now become easy, with just a click of a button.

That's not the great aspects that Evernote has attempted to create. If you have chosen to clip the whole page onto Evernote, you can use your clipped files in order to compare with items that you are currently looking at. This means that you will be able to compare reviews, prices and ratings of the same item all in one go.

Another feature that Evernote seems to have been able to apply onto the application is the ability to share their wish list with other peers. You are able to share your wish lists by sending them invitations in order to be able to see your Evernote wish list, or you can create a public link to share on any social media sight.

What this does is creates a platform for you to share with your family and friends the items that you wish for, either as a birthday present or Christmas present. Making it easier for them to buy you presents that you would actually love and use.

Of course, the use of Evernote doesn't just have to be for you. While you are with your family and friends, make sure to listen into their conversations. They might mention an item, which they wish to have for a special occasion such as birthdays or Christmas then jot it down using Evernote.

Become everyone's favorite gift-giver with the use of this nifty application!

5. Let Evernote handle the paperwork, such as when doing Insurance Claims

Insurance claims can be organized and filed through Evernote's straightforward catalogue system making it easy to track down your insurance notes from way back. With this precise categorization of insurance claims, it is almost impossible to end up doing something even remotely wrong. Throughout the years, you will have plenty of new gadgets, vehicles, property and other objects that are subject to insurance. There is a sense of safety when there is a guaranteed compensation for detailed loss, damage or illness. This requires plenty of paperwork that you simply can't store physically as it will, most often than not, deteriorate over time. Better store it in a device you can bring around that requires just a little storage space on your gadget. How do is it work? Here are some notes to consider:

1) You need to deposit all your insurance claims information in worksheets on Evernote. Having these information readily available will make it easier to get an unbiased appraisal. Even if you prefer to write it things down in person, it still isn't a problem. You can just take a photo and synchronize it to your Evernote account.

2) Evernote is key in storing tons of information you have searched online. Having shared information that you can easily access, it permits you to save time always exploring the same topic. From different types of rates, schemes and corporate contact details that are available to public access, it will be a breeze acquiring the right details.

3) Note: Insurance is a meticulous and sensitive topic when it comes to private and confidential information. There have been plenty of insurance frauds over the years and providing such security with that information isn't a forte in the Evernote front. Even with protection of some information through passwords, the best you will be able to do is to use it as means of storage.

Evernote is a perfect storage-based application that can have almost anything kept in an easy and undemanding fashion. With these notes to consider, it will give you a guide on the manageability of using Evernote even in filing insurance claims.

6. Save time and frustration when looking for important Documents

In a gradually more technologically advanced society, it makes life a little easier when dealing with the stresses of insurance and inventory of your belongings. By synchronizing all the tiny details right after purchasing something, you can either list it down on your Evernote application or you can just note it down by hand and simply upload it to your device. This will make it faster and easier to organize your topics.

Although some people prefer to jot it down automatically to Evernote, this will leave room for human error. Especially with serial numbers consisting of plenty of numbers, it might be a hassle to track down even with one mistake. So to prevent complicating things, it is preferable if you just take a photo and digitize the information. Here are some things you can use on Evernote:

1) Laptops. You can easily trace the IP (Internet Protocol) numbers of your laptop by having snaps of the serial numbers on it. Laptops are pretty important with tracking down specific models and such since once you need to repair certain bits; it is easy to provide the correct data.

2) Jewelry. You can note down the specific designs and materials used of your jewelry collection through Evernote.

3) Electronics. You can easily narrow down any researches when you have the right model and information of your electronics. Once you need the help of customer support, you don't need to bring your electronics to the store; rather you can provide photos and details of the things that can be replaced.

4) Bicycles. Same with electronics, when replacing a specific part of a bicycle, it helps to have necessary information of its parts around.

5) Furniture. Especially with moving furniture around, you can determine the size of the furniture to see if they would fit particular areas of the house without moving them at all.

6) Power tools. You can have the model numbers of the power tools as a way to show parts of the tools that need replacing without bringing it directly to the shop.

7) Insurance Documents

8) Extended Warranties

9) House Closing documents

Once you have a copy of the information of your property for inventory, all you need to do next is to email the photo directly to your Evernote email address. Afterwards, all you need to do is file those information with tags and bookmark the notes when you'll need them. You can show this information to an insurance company, making insurance claims easier to get.

7. Scan All Receipts immediately and reduce clutter

Keeping track of your business and personal expenses is something you should get used to doing. This way of organizing your spending helps you allocate where your money is going. In everyday transactions, balancing your incomes and expenses is an arduous process. If done right, it will be rewarding knowing your money is going to the right things. But with unbalanced costs, it can prove fatal especially with huge sums. Here are the different ways you can scan your receipts immediately with ease:

1) First, you need to capture the receipts. You can do this by taking a photo of it on Evernote by using the Document Camera option on the application. This will automatically create a new note with the picture of the receipt.

2) Whilst taking photos of dozens of receipt with the first option may be a little tiresome, you can always use the option of scanning your receipts directly to Evernote. You can always link your scanner to your Evernote email address so it will be easier for you to accomplish the scans.

3) You can always download a separate app on your device called "Scanner Pro". It specifically scans documents into Evernote, multiple documents at a time. For example, you want to accumulate all your receipts in one trip or in one week, you can use scanner pro to scan them all into a PDF that would be directed straight to Evernote. Otherwise, you have the option of the DocScanner app. What's good about this is that it provides minor edits to your photos to make them easier to read when scanning or taking photos of them prove difficult.

4) If you don't have the resources or just the time to scan each receipt, you can always ask the help of an online scanning service that takes your documents that need scanning , scans them and sends them to your Evernote account. They will also file them according to their tags and purpose. It's a costly option in comparison to the others, but for professionals and others are are busy to scan each receipt, this will be a huge help in organizing your finances.

8. Let Evernote help you with your Taxes

Well at least the compiling and organizing part. One of the most dreaded words in existence: taxes. Taxes are typically not something someone looks forward to, especially with deadlines nearing round. However, Evernote might just have the key to solving your tax problems. All you need to have is your files kept safely in your Evernote account as well as having the worksheets; you will be able to file your taxes on time.

1) You can save your receipts and other expenses by taking a photo of it and synchronizing it into Evernote. By directly sending it to your Evernote email address, you have nowhere to lose or forget a single receipt. This technique is better than manually typing out each receipt since it won't be exposed to human errors. Plus, this will be legitimate proof of the actual receipt.

2) Another option is to scan your receipts. By using apps that specialize in this service, such as "Scannable", you will be able to scan anything from business cards, to receipts and other documents. For your taxes, this is easy to look back and find as everything is ready for export to PDF or JPG.

3) After either saving or scanning your documents, you can tag it with the related notes. These tags will make it easier for you to look back and track down. If, for example, you want to gather all the tax documents in every month, tagging them to the month they are associated with will make it all the more easier to find in the future.

4) If your tax charts and other references are online, you can clip it by saving specific screenshots to make filing easier to accomplish. With just a click of a button, you will be able to save almost anything.

5) What to do with the final document? You can either keep it for filing or use the "Work Chat" option to create an environment where you can share your tax documents with other people. This is perfect for your accountant to look over and assess.

By using Evernote, taxes would be something to look forward to. With proper organization and planning, it will be easier and less stressful for you to engage in your business whilst paying taxes before deadlines.

9. Make better home buying decisions with Evernote

House hunting, in the end of the day could get relatively tiring to pursue. Time is consumed having to look at numerous houses in different locations and sometimes the end result doesn't pan out the way you would like it to.

So, having a hard time keeping track of all the houses you have been eye-balling?

Evernote is highly recommended for the use of this activity. Once set up with this new application, simply add a new notebook called 'House Hunting' or anything related to you looking for a house. This will be the notebook used in storing everything related in your search for a new home.

• Requirements

Before anything, be sure to know what it is you want in your new home and create a list of these items.

For example:

☐ 2 Bedroom

☐ Large Kitchen

☐ Washer and dryer

☐ Parking Space

Although, take into account that the longer the list, the more time you will need to search for your dream home. It is also important not to get too specific and to learn to be flexible with your needs.

• Hunting

Properties can be searched for everywhere. In the newspaper, your local real estate agent's window or even on the internet.

Simply use your smart devices camera to snap photos of any information not on the internet and paste it in your notebook.

Or, if ever it's on the internet, just use the Evernote Web Clipper. If you don't have this extension already, you may want to consider adding it in.

● **Plan It Out**

Make sure that once you have a list of properties that you are interested in that you are able to short list them and formulate a schedule for each location you plan to see that day.

Although, don't throw out the ones you haven't shortlisted, for they could be used in the future. To know which is shortlisted or not, add a tag on the ones you like more.

When in each location, make sure to take down notes on your Evernote, so you can compare houses once you get home and talk about it with your family.

10. Saving Time and Money on Clothes

a. For suits

This does not generally have to be for suits in general, but as an example we will use suits. If you want to save time using Evernote, you can follow these instructions

i. Create a new notebook where you will store all your clothing information, this could be your measurements or what you need to purchase for an upcoming event.

ii. When wanting to keep track of your measurements, you would need to create a table in a new note and place your measurements within the table.

iii. You could use this table as a clothing inventory as well in order to keep track of what you do have in order to save on items that you shouldn't need to buy.

iv. You could also create a checklist when you go shopping for your clothing.

b. For ordering things online

What the problems with wanting to purchase items online is that after a while, if it isn't properly saved somewhere, you will tend to forget where you found that item.

• Take pictures of some of the same items that you want to purchase and use Evernote to place those items in one area. This could be used for comparing which item is the better buy

• When placing what you want to buy in a folder, you won't have to search for those items over again in order to check the information. Using Evernote saves time on having to re-do searches.

c. Kids sizes and measurements

This is a similar concept to that of saving time and money on clothes for suits. If you are a parent of numerous kids and want to purchase clothes for them while they aren't with you. Evernote could provide you the platform for storing such information.

Creating a new notebook on your kids clothing, you can simply place a table where you place all your kid's sizes starting from hat sizes to their shoe sizes.

Creating a checklist as well on what they have asked for you to purchase could do you justice when in the clothing store.

11. Always give the perfect gift

The words you always want to hear when gifting: "That is exactly what I was looking for". Create a note for important people in your life and jot down things about them, such as their kids names ages and gender, hobbies, etc. Then when it comes time for gifting you will know exactly what to gift.

Here are tips in being able to create your very own Gift Database with the use of Evernote

• Capturing Gifts and Notes

Using Evernote, you will need the ability to listen to what your peers are saying and what they may be wishing to get for the future and having the ability to capturing that need into your Evernote notebook.

□ Paper

If ever you have a piece of paper where you have jotted down the title of this new book that your best friend has been eye balling, make sure you take a photo of it when no one is looking and paste it into Evernote.

□ Web-Page

For any web-inspired gifts, this is where your Evernote Web Clipper will come in handy. Highlight the important aspects such as name, price and picture and hit the bookmark button in order to clip the full page. This will allow you to go back to the link in the future and it could be used as a tool to compare pricing.

12. Maintain your home better by tracking all your maintenance activities

Having trouble keeping track of important home information such as your records, receipts and invoices?

Well, Evernote has got you covered.

So here are tips and tricks on how to use Evernote to your advantage when keeping track of your home items:

• Scanning Your Documents and Receipts

If behooves you to keep track of all the work you've done on your house and when. All you need to do is to take photos of all your receipts or documents and keep them filed into their own notebook in Evernote.

It will be easier to find each receipt or document once it is placed in its own folder for future use. Furthermore, you can create a reminder for a service followup. For example, create a reminder a year from now to perform an A/C checkup, to clean the gutters, or to do flush your water heater.

• Manual Maintenance

When wanting to maintain your home and you have found the perfect website that tells you how. Just use your Evernote Web Clipper to place it into a new note for when you need it.

If you can't seem to find your copy online, then take pictures of your paper copy to put into Evernote.

• Home Maintenance Routines

A home needs daily, weekly, monthly and weekly maintenance in order to keep it in tip top shape.

Create reminders that would tell you when something needs to be checked or looked into. For example: a reminder every six months to get your car checked would help you reduce any damages in the long run. Or, getting a reminder to do the months cleaning of your whole house to keep any dirt or unnecessary items at bay.

Creating a checklist as well could help you give an idea of the numerous places to get things done within your household that you have noticed. For example, you find a light bulb not working on your porch, add that to your checklist. This will serve as a reminder on what to do during your free time.

• Home Inventory

Taking down a list of items within your household could act as the perfect way to avoid any unnecessary purchases in the future. More importantly, you might need it one day for insurance claim purposes.

13. Save on Auto Maintenance by tracking repairs meticulously

Do you remember if you paid for lifetime balancing? Do you remember where? Do you remember if you paid for flat warranty on your tires and if so where? Do you remember when was the last time you flushed your brakes or had a full tuneup? Unless you always take your car to the dealer chances are it will take you a while to recall all that information. With Evernote it can be auotomated and recalled in seconds.

By keeping track and recording all your invoices and maintenance you will be able to do proactive repairs on your auto instead of waiting until it breaks making it worse. So the question is now how do you keep maintenance records on Evernote?

1) One way is to ask for the repair store to kindly send you a digital copy of your receipt through your email. This saves you the hassle of transferring the hard copy of the receipt to your Evernote.

2) If ever you end up receiving a hard copy of your receipts, scan it through the "Document" camera option on the application.

3) You can also have the option of normally typing the receipt details but it isn't reliable and it's time consuming.

4) Always tag all your invoices immediately.

5) Set reminders if applicable. For example, if you just completed a brake job schedule your next brake job for the recommended time. If you just completed an oil change set a reminder.

Once you start to keep track of your auto maintenance you will be able to:

1) Quickly look back at the latest receipt to check when the last time you gave your auto a check up. This is useful just in case the maintenance staff asks.

2) Create a detailed maintenance record when selling your car. You will automatically flick through Evernote swiftly with a click of a few buttons.

3) A copy of your auto's manual can easily be viewed to inspect any auto reports your manufacture may mention.

4) If anything, it will give remind you of the characteristics to certain accidents your auto may come across. You can snap photos of scratched hoods, missing parts and even damaged paint.

5) Keep track of your real maintenance expenses.

It is extremely satisfying that Evernote has the option to tag certain photos and group them into specific purposes. If you're looking for records in a certain shop, you have it at your fingertips. If you're finding past accidents you've encountered when it comes to the back of your auto, you can search certain that specific tag.

13.b Create maintenance reminders

Create reminders for your regular scheduled maintenance items. For example, when you buy new tires create new note with a reminder with an estimate on when you should start looking for new tires, say two years from now. Do this for Brakes, Tires, Tire rotations, Tire balancing, fluid flushes, tune-ups, filters, etc.

14. Take Charge of your Health by Keeping Medical Records

A digital copy of your medical record will be extremely useful in the long run. What happens is that over time, the accumulation of your frequent trips to your doctor for check ups, the receipts, the certain prescriptions you need and the results of tests will be vital in ensuring your physical health. You need something that would gather all these information in a medium that is a compromise for all. Why not Evernote? Evernote does just that. It digitalizes your notes in a medium that will make researching and assembling information straightforward.

1. Medical records

Having an easy access and appropriate storage of every necessary information of your major check ups and results is a blessing. Information you receive can be passed on from one expert to another without difficulty. You will be able to trace back every single medical situation you have gone through and it will be a breeze to uncover. For example, even by noting down minute details of slight pains, frequent headaches and unusual sprains, you can give a comprehensive record of your medical history that you can easily submit to your medical practitioner.

2. Receipts

Scanning and updating your medical receipts is a piece of cake. By downloading specific apps that cater to scanning your medical receipts and other related documents, you will have a digital platform to track down your overall spending.

3. Prescriptions

In case of buying more prescriptions, you now have the option of looking back to the medication you've used before and use Evernote to track down what you need. For example, certain medicine you took before on how to cure migraines. This will save you the bother of researching it all up again on the Internet or check up with the doctor on whether it will personally help you.

4. X-rays, scans, etc.

Keeping a record of your medical results will allow you medical practitioners to assess your current health situation with ease.

15. Always know where to go eat out

With the food culture increasing in popularity and innovation in the fast few years, everything about the conception, the process and the end product of food is widely followed and analyzed. People use social media and outlets to criticize and document food in all its glory as a way to market different type of food, provide reviews as well as the food culture in relation to art.

People have intense fascination with food, it is a necessity that we literally can't live without and he dynamics of the food business is developing over the years. Evernote has kept a steady partnership with features that keep up to the growing demand and changes that food and technology has to offer. What does Evernote have to offer?

1. Great meals can be explored via Evernote on a steady Internet connection. Famous food bloggers use the Internet as an outlet to review and promote recipes and restaurants that boast food with exquisite taste and novel experiences. This career path is no joke as food enthusiasts will continuously update their website with new things to write. Evernote plays a vital role, as it is a link between you and these bloggers. The search option on Evernote allows you to search for specific ingredients, global cuisine and dish names.

You can even track down and save restaurants that you want to try out in the future or restaurants you'd like to come back to. Locations of these restaurants are accessible making it simple and efficient.

2. Great wine can be listed and liked for future references. Usually you would enjoy the meal and wine and end up forgetting what you ordered in the first place. With Evernote, you have the option of pressing the plus sign on the app, which then allows you to add a title to your wine. You can trace it back and have the perfect wine over and over again.

3. A menu list to find cooking ideas is right around the corner. If there is a recipe you're interested in trying out, you can effortlessly attach it to your Evernote cookbook. You have the option to check it out later on.

16. Keep Product manuals at your fingertips by throwing them away

Admit it, when buying a product you would either flip through the manuals or just ignore them completely. Manuals are designed to explain the purpose and use of the product in absolute detail. That means a step-by-step account on even the most obvious and unmistakable things to do and not to do. It is perfectly understandable to pay no attention. Throw it away you don't need it, it will just cause discomfort taking up unnecessary storage space. Or do you?

Sometimes, you will encounter a problem that you just can't solve. You look for the manual, but alas, you remember that it's probably in a pile dump hidden somewhere. You scan through the Internet looking for forums and threads that will specifically help your certain situation. Alas again, nothing to be found. Even spending hours on end researching and get the answer you think you need, it's not entirely what you expected.

This causes more and more frustration and you just end up the product back for assistance with a migraine and stress tablets.

Evernote prevents this from happening. It has features that make any manual inconvenience a thing of the past. How is that possible?

1. You can either take the time to scan each individual manual page by using apps that specialize in this feature. Afterwards, you will need to synchronize it to your Evernote tags and notes.

2. The best option is to use your physical manual as a guide to find PDF (portable document format) copies your manuals and download them accordingly. By storing the PDF file into your Evernote account, it will be more efficient to look back and find topics that you need to read on.

3. Note: If the product you have recently purchased is new in the market, track down the PDF manual as soon as possible. Usually when it comes to electronics, updated versions are constantly refreshing the product. It is more difficult to find the original soft copy of your manual a few months or years later especially when the product has manuals that have the latest versions of it.

17. Always know what to cook (Using Evernote Food)

Have you ever sat down with a cup of hot cocoa on your hand overlooking a passer-by and contemplated on what your most memorable meal was? You remember the taste, the experience and the innovative mixture of ingredients, but can't quite pinpoint the name or even where you've tried it. Have you ever passed by a new restaurant or bistro you promised to check out, but haven't quite gotten around to it? Well, Evernote Food basically helps you locate your favorite meals are, aids in finding the newest or hidden restaurants you are dying to visit and helps you keep safe old family recipes that have been passed on from generation to generation.

What is Evernote food exactly? It's the perfect application to bring around for food enthusiasts that drive your curiosity and interest. You not only record your favorite meals are, their recipes or their location, but it helps you keep the memories that go with them.

1. Evernote Food makes it easier for you to search recipes across the Internet that you can save and try in the future. There's a feature in the application hat allows you to clip the recipes you like and save them into an option called "My Cookbook".

2. My Cookbook retrieves any recipes you have saved and can be easily accessible in your times of need. Whatever you clipped and saved in My Cookbook, it is directly linked with Evernote Food. Add a couple of tags to your recipes to catalogue them into their different ingredients, styles and levels, then you're good to go.

3. Evernote Food keeps a list of the restaurants you've always wanted to visit. You can locate restaurants around your area and if anything catches your eye, add them to your list in Evernote Food. Did I mention that you could even find restaurants around the world? This is ideal for you to plan ahead where you'd like to go when you're out on a trip. There's an in-built map choice that specifically shows you where the restaurant is located, therefore you won't end up getting lost on your way. This can also help with restaurant or bistro hopping.

18. Keep Important Documents Handy, and save closet space!

Important documents are completely necessary in applying and verifying various situations. There are plenty of scammers and frauds in the world today that the government and different agencies are restricting false documents and identities. By having these important documents at the ready, it will be easier to move around and conduct business and daily activities without inconvenience.

1. Passport

Once you've lost your passport or had it stolen on your recent flight to an exotic country, it is a pain in the behind to process a new one. There needs to be supporting documents to prove that they really are valid, it is a hassle applying for a new one an picking it up, et cetera. You can add documents to Evernote by scanning your passport details and import those PDFs into Evernote or use Evernote's very own "Scan To Evernote" feature via Image Capture if you have a Mac.

2. Drivers license

After successfully scanning your documents, such as your driver's license, into Evernote, you can easily search it. Go to the search bar and type whatever you're looking for then the search options would give you results of documents with that certain topic. A digitized copy is manageable to use in transactions. If you need to send a soft copy of your driver's license, you can just send a forwarded scanned copy of it than go through the bother of scanning and sending.

3. Car title

Your car title, for instance, is advisable to keep on Evernote. You can legitimize your ownership by keeping them organized. You can tag them according to their title and use. This way, if you forgot the title of your car, you can add tags such as "car title", car brand and/or year purchased.

4. House closing docs

If you follow these steps, it will be easy to track down the necessary information. House closing documents are also useful to have on Evernote. You don't need to keep it stored in folders up on the shelf. On Evernote, it will be easily located with a click of a few buttons. Voila! Simple and productive! It truly is a mandatory accessory for everyday transactions!

19. Make Use of Extended Warranties

Having a hard time making use of the warranty and extended warranties on the items you purchase because you don't know where you place the receipt? They can be real sticklers about having the actual receipt before they make good on their warranties.

Well, say goodbye to your troubles.

Evernote could also act as your database when keeping track of all the warranties you have on each item. For example: purchasing a new mac provides you a warranty that is granted for a year. If anything happens between that time, you could use your warranty to save you on expenses.

Here's what you need to remember to do when wanting to make the most out of your warranties.

- **Purchase, then scan right away**

   Make it a habit that as soon as you purchase an item that comes with warranty, that you take a picture or scan that document for the future. If ever your purchased electronic or any other product gets damaged in the future and you don't know where you placed the warranty slip, you could use your scanned file as evidence.

   It isn't that hard to remember to scan your documents and in the end, it could serve to save your life in terms of expenses.

- **Create reminders**

   It is also a good idea to place a reminder telling yourself when which item would end its warranty period. This could serve as a reminder to check up on your products condition and see if you could use the warranty card in order to ripen its condition.

- **Taking Advantage of Promises**

   This goes in light of what your plumber, mechanic or roofer has promised you that they would achieve. If you have a deal of what they aim to fix or if they have promised that the problem wouldn't surface in five years. Then it would be easier to take on this warranty if anything happens down the line.

   For example: a plumber's company could guarantee that the item they have now installed into your faucet will work for the next two years. If not, then replacement will be on the cost of the company and not to you. If they had this in writing, you could show this if ever the item ends up getting broken.

20. Plan your wedding, and stay sane!

The Evernote productivity isn't only ideal for daily life and work-related activities; it is also perfect for planning a wedding. Of course, a wedding is a huge event, one that caters to various tasks and nitty-gritty detail. If you are busy and decide to hire a wedding planner, it is completely understandable. Although, planning with the wedding planner is still going to be necessary. But if you are someone who wants to plan your perfect day and who is passionate about experiencing this once in a lifetime (fingers crossed) event, then Evernote is what you should consider using.

Evernote is excellent for (planning) a wedding. Here's why:

- Identifying and organizing your guest list becomes a headache. You will need to make sure that you have invited your family and friends, as well as your partner's entourage. Ensure that you haven't missed out an important guest. Through Evernote, it will be easy to track everyone down.

- Through the web-clipping feature for Evernote, you can take pictures and screenshots of designs and decorations that you might want to include in your wedding. You can mash these all up into a single document for you to later reflect and compare.

- You don't even need to look at websites to clip inspirations, you can take photos of objects you see in a shop and use it in your Evernote account.

- One benefit of Evernote is that you can keep track of everyone's email address and other information making it easier for you to send invites and Thank You notes.

- Evernote allows you to communicate directly to various people in charge of specific parts of your wedding. For instance, you can email the catering regarding what food you want served and how you want it served. This saves time, making you do more at a quicker pace.

- The best feature in organizing is the tags you will put on everything you document on Evernote. Although all your wedding details are stored in one document, perhaps entitled "My Wedding", you can have notes with relative tags. It is easier to locate and easier to work with.

21. Save your focus and read it later

In life, as you grow older, you will realize that there is not enough time in your day to do everything you want to do. Reading included.

Our daily experiences may force us to be bombarded with numerous news articles, fashion magazines or the next great book that your friends suggest for you to read. This is great! You have enough material to read for the rest of your life! Although, that's the problem, having the option to read so many books may deem a challenge when you have no time to.

Instead of letting another article or book pass you by, use Evernote to be able to read it later without having to lose the book name, title or link. A solution has been created for your reading pleasure!

Now, you're probably wondering what you have to do to achieve. The answer is simple and there are two solutions:

1. Use Evernote and clip and save articles that you have come across and are interested in reading on your desktop through the use of your Web Clipper. You can easily reach and understand the genres of each article by applying the tag and cataloging feature that Evernote has. Whether it's a business article or a novel.

2. Use Pocket with Evernote. Using pocket provides the perfect aspect in discovering and saving the items that you don't have time to read at the moment. Just as its name, all you do is pocket the articles or materials you want to read later, even without the Internet connection.

As you wait in line, take a look at articles and save them for when you can relax and read. You can save from browsers such as Twitter and Flipboard and it doesn't stop there. You can save videos too!

Getting tired of all the advertisements on your web page while reading an article? Well, what Pocket is capable of doing, is rid all your saved articles from those annoying ads.

Even when you have finished an article, you don't have to delete it right away. Especially, recipes, you can archive these materials for future use. Just Share it from Pocket to Evernote and the search for these materials will be swift and easy.

22. Gift Ideas – Capture Wish Lists and Gift Ideas

When in search for the perfect present that you know your friend, lover or relative will love, and a lot of thought and attention needs to be put into it. Even those who are so attentive to giving gifts it can be tough keeping track of the 10 people you need to buy Christmas gifts for.

Use Evernote to your advantage when wanting to keep track of what to spend for whom with these tips:

- **Planning a Joint Gifting**

  If it wasn't mentioned in previous articles, you should know that Evernote is able to provide for you the option of sharing your notes with your peers.

  Have you ever considered buying an expensive present with someone else to lessen the burden of the cost?

  Well, with that feature, you can share your gift ideas with more than one person and in the end come to a joint decision on what it is you are going to buy for the birthday girl or boy.

  If ever you are a premium user, you can grant modification rights for Shared Notebooks so everyone that is participating in the joint gift could contribute their opinions on what to purchase too!

- **Always Be Wary**

  This basically means pay attention to what your family or friends are saying when you are around them. Even if you are having a casual conversation with them, they may spill out some details on what they want on their birthday. This is the best opportunity to take out your smart device or portable laptop, log into Evernote and take down what they wanted!

  You'll definitely be the best gift giver by the end of the year.

- **Remember the Present, Forget the Date**

  Use the reminder feature in Evernote to be able to remind you when you need to prepare the present and the day you have to give it. What would be a bummer is if you had picked out the perfect birthday present for the person, but through your busy schedule, you have forgotten that today is the day!

Forget no more!

Chapter 4:
Leverage Collaboration with Evernote at Work

1. Compile Research and Share Notes

Reading this Evernote book, there may have been mentions of being able to share your notes. It may have been mentioned once very briefly and it may have been mentioned in a way that seems like there is only one way to share your notes with others.

However, there is more than one way to share your notes to those who need to receive it:

01. Share your Notes with the use of the Work Chat

a. Select that specific note that you want to share from your notes list

b. If you are on your desktop, then simply click the **Share** button or select the **Work Chat** button in order to continue. If you are on your iOS device, then click on the **Speech Bubble** with the arrow or tap the **Share Button** (which looks like three joined dots) that is placed on top of the screen for Android devices.

c. You now are able to change the permission levels to either *'Can edit and invite'*, *'Can edit'* or *'Can view.*

d. Add at least one of the e-mail addresses or contact, type a message if you wish and click **Send**

02. Sharing a Public Link (otherwise known as URL) to a Note

● **Windows**: Click the pointing down arrow on the Share button in the menu, click **Copy Share URL**

● **Mac**: Same with windows, but you click **Copy Public Link**

- **iPhone, iPad or iPod**: Open note, tap Share in options menu and **Copy Link**

- **Android**: Tap options menu, then **More Sharing**, tap **Post a Link**, then **Copy URL**

- **Web**: Click the arrow pointing down in the Share button, and select **Link**

03. Emailing that Note

- **Windows**: Click the arrow pointing down in the Share button and select **Send by Email**

- **Mac**: Select **Notes** > **More Sharing** > **Email a Copy** that is displayed in the Evernote menu bar.

- **iPhone, iPad or iPod**: Open note, tap Options menu which looks like three dots at the bottom of the screen > **Share** > **Mail**

- **Android**: Options menu (top of the screen) > **More Sharing** > **Share Static Note** > Enter recipient > **Send**

- **Web**: Click arrow pointing down in Share button and select **Email**

2. Track Projects Large and Small

Evernote is workplace friendly and supports any projects, from the point of having it commence to the very last edits and everything in between. Being able to keep track of all your projects, whether it is big or small is an essential when maintaining your progress. It would be most unfortunate if you spent 30 minutes to an hour just looking for the project that you set aside a month ago.

So, here is how to learn to use the notes and notebook framework that Evernote provides in order to plan and manage even the most complicated projects that you would undergo.

- **Capturing Each Steps into Your Notes**

By starting a new note, you could capture all the minutes of your meeting that is precious information, get on track on what needs to be accomplished with the use of the checklist or create a proposal to share to your team.

Even if you aren't on your computer you could use the Evernote app on your smart device to type out little notes and capture photos you may need for the future.

Evernote doesn't limit you to the amount of notes or projects you can take on!

• Organizing your Work in Notebooks

In order to keep your notes and photos organized, then consider making a project notebook in order to create the home for that specific topic. When you are able to collect all the parts that your project needs in one area, you won't have to hunt around anymore for all the components and waste time. Everything you need to accomplish your projects will be within your fingertips.

• Connecting with Your Work Mates

Need to show your classmates the work? Or have to work with someone for a project, but having a hard time reaching them?

Well, Evernote has incorporated the idea of a Work Chat. This handy feature allows you to share you project with your friends or the team you need to collaborate with. It will definitely allow the ultimate effort from everyone as they are alongside you as you work.

These are the basics to know how to handle all the projects with the use of Evernote.

3. Never drop the ball by tracking tasks and to do lists

If you can't achieve to managing tasks or reminding yourself of the tasks that you need to accomplish then your life may seem a bit chaotic when your boss asks you where your week's assignment is and you have completely forgot to finish it.

So, how can you achieve to manage both the tasks for your career as well as your personal life?

There are numerous tools out there that could provide aid when trying to maintain your productivity. But, even with all the tools the solution to creating the best system for yourself.

As the workplace is the best place for you to create and grow ideas, Evernote has your back when needing a central area to store all these tasks that is required from you, may it be during work or even at home.

Here's how you can accomplish this with Evernote in

01. A Single Note to Rule Them All – Creating a new note for specific tasks could help keep it managed. Place a title of your projects name and use the note to write a description of what the project is or create checklists for what needs to be accomplished for that specific project.

02. Check – Manage your tasks on the go with the use of the checklist feature that Evernote has. Be sure to check your task list and tick out everything that you have accomplished so that you won't waste time having to do that task again.

03. Tick the Accomplished – As soon as your task has been complete, then tick your checklist

04. Different Categories – If you have numerous tasks for different projects, make sure to separate the titles and choose different fonts or colors for these items.

05. Linking Tasks – If ever you see a pattern that many of the tasks that you need to accomplish are related to work that you have done somewhere else, then you can connect them together with the use of note links.

06. Shortcuts – When you want to spend less time trying to look for certain tasks to check, then you can create shortcuts.

4. CRM (Customer Relationship Management): Never forget a face, or their kids names

Consider making Evernote your best friend when it comes to your career. How can this be achieved? Well, use Evernote when trying to keep track of all the important business people or clients that you meet with everyday in order to provide the best service or product for them.

Do you work in a bakery that promotes specialized wedding cakes? When you meet with a client, you can use it to jot down what they want the cake to look like or any specifications and use the reminder to tell you when it needs to be done.

Are you based in a law firm? Usually, some employees may be tasked with having to meet important clients and these clients may proceed to providing you with valuable information. So using the notes that Evernote can provide for you, you will be able to keep track of what they're saying in order to rely the information to your firm once the meeting is over.

Even using Evernote as a way to create minutes of the meetings that you attend to for those secretaries and sharing them to your boss once it is accomplished allows for a simple and quick way to passing information.

Create these notes in order to make your career manageable.

Here is how you could use Evernote to your business needs:

- **Save Every Detail about them**

  When you meet someone or when profiling, you can simply place it in a new note provided with any other important information such as their name, their birthday, why they are important as well as a photo of what they look like.

  As these records are kept they can be easily edited in the future, if ever their likes, dislikes or hobbies tend to change

- **Share Your Spoils**

  Consider also sharing this information with your work mates. Imaging it like this, if you were the boss of a five-man team and you are required to make a proposition for an important man, sharing this profile with the five others on your team could serve as the quickest way to share the information needed.

• Add value with reminders

Using reminders in real life is just as important as using it for your career. You are probably demanded more for your business than real life and in order to stay on top of all these deadlines and demands that is required of you, it is beneficial to set numerous reminders.

For example: If you have a meeting to attend then set a reminder as well as write down what the meeting is for, who will be attending it and what may be required from you during this meeting in order for you to be able to prepare the requirements before the meeting at hand. If your manager has asked you to come to the set meeting and prepare a presentation, a reminder could set you on when it should be accomplished as well as the checklist could act as what should be placed in your presentation.

Rule of thumb: don't forget the importance of what a reminder could offer you.

• Do big things by remembering little things

It may not be obvious to you, but remembering the little information such as where your client loves to eat, hang out or their favorite beverages could be a huge advantage when trying to pursue them for your business venture.

Think about it this way. They would really appreciate working with a business that remember which wines they like. If you took your client to a seafood restaurant and they are allergic to shell-fish, it could end up a disaster on your end and all hope of redeeming that client would be small to none.

Try to implement the Evernote into your business. Do you know why the Chinese business men are so organized? Because they take advantage of WeChat, which is an application that allows you to chat to anyone in the world just by connecting to the internet. So, like the Chinese, use Evernote as your advantage to get ahead in the business world. Make sure your employees are well-educated about this new technology and improve with it.

5. Store Invoices, Procedure Manuals & Run your Small Business from Evernote

Struggling to handle your business? Evernote could do more than just provide you an area to keep your notes and reminders, it could act as a support for your business. Finding a hard time comprehending how it can do so? Well, here's how Evernote has been created for your business needs:

- Structuring your Business Workflow

Tasks that have been assigned for who, to-do lists for your store managers and daily recaps or reminders for you employees could be shared within your work space through the use of Evernote. With the use of shared notebooks, each employee could see and check the numerous items that they would be responsible for.

- Electronic Filing Cabinet

Any and all invoice, credit card receipts, alcohol licenses and employee files could be scanned and documented within your Evernote application, this allows them to be easily reached and accessed, especially for the managers use.

Whether a chef is looking at price inflations on ingredients, accountant is looking for receipts or the manager is looking for important documentation for an off-site contractor, Evernote provides easy access to all information need for the business. Simply type in a few key words into the search box to find the document.

- Standardized and Centralized Training and Hiring Procedures

This could be advantageous especially for restaurants. A business like this could efficiently organize new hire documents, record notable incidents that need to be looked into as well as review employees on a day-to-day basis. Each employee under you could gain their own profiles that would possess all their achievements as well as wrong doings. Issues are easily noted.

You could say that Evernote is Human Resources lifesaver.

- Preparation

As it had said in the previous section, it could be used when collaborating in projects. For business, this could be when you are planning to open another store for your business. It could hold precious information as to the light bulbs that the restaurant require and when in the hardware store, it would make your life easier when you already know what items need to be purchased.

6. Document Processes and Workflows

Having the ability to document the important tasks that will be able to keep your business forward could create a great practice for professionals, whether in a team or as an individual. Keeping notes on all your business workflows will make it a lot easier when you need to remember what to do, sharing these tasks to those who need to know what to do, and making sure that what is written is understood.

Here are some of the ways that Evernote could help aid document your different workflows:

• Documenting the Simple Procedures

Evernote could be used when creating non-screen-based workflows written down such as the procedures as how to proceed when dealing with follow-up phone calls to your clients or the procedures that don't require much detailing explanation, like sending an email.

When creating these workflows, then use the checkbox and numbered list in order to set the outline specific steps and any other information that could be further explained.

• Documenting the Complicated Workflows

For any workflow that requires detailed actions, pictures could be better than your words. The idea behind being able to combine your text and images could be beneficial when you want to achieve a minimize confusion so that those who are not accustomed to the procedures could complete the task correctly, with swiftness and ease.

You could combine Evernote with other applications and documenting complicated workflows could include either one of the following two:

a. Skitch with Evernote

With the use of Skitch, it allows you to grab any screenshots you have taken, annotate it and send it directly to your Evernote application to document, store or share. Skitch also provides the feature to highlight all the details you will need for those who will be doing the workflow in order to easily accomplish the task.

b. Clarify with Evernote

This is a great tool when you want to document multi-step workflows on your computer. You have the ability to take multiple screenshots with the use of Clarify, annotate each screenshot, organize these into a series of steps and add any further text you may need for each item.

7. Use Evernote To Brainstorm And Present From Your Notes

Presenting your notes and showcasing them in a meeting are two totally different processes. From people who prefer the manual note taking, handwritten notes will then need to be transferred, encoded and neatly organized in a legible and understandable manner. This is an arduous process, not to mention time consuming.

Evernote is a great medium to brainstorm and present your notes directly. What it does is it collects various notes that you've hand selected on Evernote and collates them. With a click of button, you will be able to present it to large or small groups of people in a simple and comprehensible arrangement. Why should you use it?

1. Quick presentation of notes. There is a button on every note you write on Evernote. Itis in the icon of a projection screen and with the click of the button, it will present any note you have opened. You don't need to change the format at all. All you have to do now is just scroll around that certain note whilst explaining it.

2. Think you don't enough freedom to customize your notes? Worry not, if the default setting is too plain for you, you can control how your note is presented. At default, Evernote presents your notes in a long scrollable note. However, you can choose to cut it up into smaller sections. With some simple navigation options, you will be a master in no time.

3. You can always alter the settings when you present your notes. As well as highlight contents that are of importance and change the displayed font sizes to accommodate your listeners.

4. How about brainstorming? You can set up another monitor and edit the note on the laptop screen whilst it is being displayed on a larger screen. What you have to do is to choose the "Change Screen" button when you are presenting your topic and then select what monitor your shows the presentation. This is a perfect way of brainstorming, whatever you have discussed, it is in the proper medium to downlaod as a PDF file ready to send to all the members of the meeting.

8. Take Notes you can actually read afterwards

My handwriting is horrible. I usually have to interpret, rather than read what I wrote down. However my typing is not so bad. The problem is you end up with a thousand notepad files everywhere. Not so if you take notes with Evernote.

Note taking is something every great employee and employer has to do at least at every waking moment of their lives. Our attention span and memory is limited with various problems and things to remember; it just doesn't seem feasible to memorise each detail. With business meetings, taking notes is just an inch more important. Each deal and discussion can't be repeated and manually writing down notes in paper can be a bother when there are papers flying about. There is a high chance your vital notes are mixed with other documents. The result? A stress filled afternoon searching for them. If done correctly, Evernote as a medium for note taking is a life saver.

- Research way to sync with Google calendar or outlook. Google calendar is being used by millions of people at an increasing rate. It's simple and user-friendly application is perfect for experts and amateurs alike. Powerbot for Evernote is a perfect link to Google calendar. It connects your notes and documents in Evernote directly to your schedule in Google calendar.

  ☐ First you will need to go to the powerbot application website where you give authorization to your Google account. It will then be allowed to access all your data to make planning your notes effortless.

• IFTTT perhaps? IFTTT stands for "If This Then That", it is a service that can help you attach online tasks that will post the same document on numerous social websites. It's a domino effect wherein taking action in one channel will then automatically saves that action in others that are linked to it. This is ideal in a business set up where you can just send your notes or discussions to different sites and applications.

• Take a photo of white boarding sessions.

☐ Taking photos through Evernote of whiteboarding sessions can save you an immense amount of time and energy. You won't need to depend on memory to recreate the entire discussion in your head, rather having the exact replica of everything discussed is a huge advantage. This will also double as proof if ever there are conflicting opinions on the meeting regarding the whit board sessions.

9. Declutter Your Inbox

Emailing tons of documents from important files to receipts is an everyday occurrence. You will have automatically sent a lot of your information into your Evernote email address for you to organize and sort out in the future. Typically, emails are a means of communication business details and personal conversations. However, even contemplating on organizing those details can prove to be discouraging.

1. Move action items out of your email and into Evernote. What you need to do:

a. Forward your current email to your Evernote address. You can do this by going to the "Account Info" area of Evernote and find your Evernote email mentioned on the Settings on Evernote Web and the Sync tab for Evernote.

b. To move your email into specific notebooks, the "@" symbol should lead to the title of notebook. If you want to add a tag, you need to include the "#" sign.

2. Move reference material to Evernote.

    a. Email into Evernote will help you counter this by allowing you to declutter massive amounts of mail as well as immediately segregating your daily and weekly incoming email into specific notebooks.

    b. It will also gather receipts received in order to make it easier to file in the future. If you have emails that you don't really intend to read or arrange, it would archive any old emails directly which you can always go back to in the future. When planning for a trip, Evernote would be able to collect details of that trip.

10. Eat business cards for lunch

Did you save the 75 business cards from everybody you met at last year's trade show? Did you jot down a few notes about each person you met? Did you set reminders to follow up? All of this can be automated with Evernote.

The more your business networks grow, the more you see yourself stacking up mountains of business cards. This purpose to have connections of people from different fields that you can contact if ever an opportunity arises. You can't always bring around all those cards in thick and bulky holders. It is amazing to even fit a significant amount in your wallet. Evernote makes it ideal for you have a medium to keep all these contacts on the ready without the inconvenience. This is how it works:

    1. In order to scan the business cards, you will need to first of all connect your device into the Internet.

    2. Next you will need to activate the camera button at the bottom of the screen. It can be a "Photos" icon in the home screen for some devices and others would see a "+" icon depending on your phone.

    3. For apple users, the camera will automatically detect whether it is a business card or not. Once detected, it will then capture the photo, just make sure that the edges are within the screen. If ever it doesn't get detected, turn the Auto mode on the upper right corner. For androids users, you will need to manually swipe it to "Business Card" mode.

4. Sometimes the photo won't exactly come out perfect; it depends really on the background of your card and the light reflecting. Make sure it is placed in a contrasting background to the wallpaper of your card.

5. After capturing the photo, Evernote will automatically fill in all the necessary detail, from the person's name, job title, company and contact information. You can even add notes at the bottom to write how you met or their relations to you, etc. just so you will remember in the future.

6. Things to note:

• Always review your card. There are times where they would automatically place the wrong information in the wrong detail.

• You can save your contacts automatically by tapping the name and click "General" then "Camera" and finally click "Save to Contacts" on the "Business Cards folder. This way, you can just keep the hard copy of the business cards at home and use Evernote as your business reference.

Chapter 5:
Double your Blogging productivity with Evernote

1. Blogging Support

Whether using a blogging site as a means to earn money or just for the fun of it, blogging is the perfect way to reach out information and opinions to thousands of people around the world. It is a growing trend moving towards informal and formal usage. You have so many ideas in your head and you're constantly inspired on the go. What better way to manage your blog ideas into one app, say Evernote. What Evernote aims to achieve is that you will be able to write different notes about different blog ideas that you can keep until you are ready to publish the finished product. How does it work?

1. Get a template of making blog notes on Evernote. You can set this up by yourself according to your own preferences. The most basic thing to remember when writing a blogging template is: the title (what you are writing about), the overall theme (what part of the content are you focusing on) the content (what exactly are you going to include in this post complete with bullet pointed answers). This will help you finalize your topics later on.

2. All you have to do is to copy your blog template to your blog notebook with a tag relating to your different concepts of your posts. You can make each blog idea distinct by naming it according to what its content is. This way you can have plenty of ideas that you just need to jot down that you can refer to later.

3. Writing your blog on Evernote is extremely easy. Just write all the things you have included in your template and constantly work on it and edit it until perfection. Once you are satisfied with the end result, you can now upload it on Evernote.

4. You can literally copy and paste whatever you've written on Evernote into your blog of choice. Of course, you will need to alter its settings such as the font, size, etc. of the words to your liking. It's not necessary, if you want a simple blog, then copy and paste will do.

2. Clip websites

Have you ever came across a situation where you find an inspiration online that would look great on your website? Before that inspiration turns to dust, Evernote allows you to Clipwebsites. What this means is that you can take parts of different websites that have caught your attention and you can use it later as influence to new blog ideas. It's really simple; this is what you should do:

1. Find a blog worth searching for and clip certain parts of the sites. Use the Web Clipper feature on Evernote to start extracting some sites. You can cut parts of the site and review it offline to improve productivity.

2. Once you've gotten the screenshots of the sites, you can annotate the clips to personalize and add new inputs on that specific inspiration.

3. Finally, you can share it to individuals or a group of people. This way it will be easier to discuss the specifics to your team or business group.

How is this helpful?

1. Flick through blogs that have are constantly an inspiration to you. There are plenty of blogs and websites online that have blown you away and you just want to mirror their work but add a bit of your flare. It doesn't mean that you are completely copying their work; you can use it and alter it to make an innovative and new outlook to the same idea. You should clip the website(s) for future references.

2. Evernote gives you the ability to copy websites by screenshotting it and alternating it to your liking. You may have already thought of ideas similar to the web clips and by looking at other people developing that identical idea, it supports your idea of it.

3. Evernote Clipwebsites are perfect for you to clip certain facts and quotes that you have been meaning to include in your own website. You don't need to write it down or memorize it word for word. This will allow you to look back at your Evernote clips in one medium than having to search them separately. It's a simple way of working with what you have in the same browser that makes it efficient and worth it.

3. Annotate Photos

Skitch is the ideal Evernote feature to annotate specific parts of your web clips or screenshots. Skitch helps you comprehend texts and articles that make it people understand it better. Perfect for presentations or group projects, screenshots will show you what the articles are and the annotations would help further explain it.

People are more comfortable with seeing blogs that have images and diagrams than solely depending on words and paragraphs. Skitch will also help better illustrate your stories that will be understood by many. Sometimes words can't directly and effectively impact the reader, there needs to be aspects of imagery.

1. First, you'll need to launch skitch on the device you will be using. Every document that you are using has the same skitch tools to alter the document. It either adds a text, shape or arrow. Better yet, it offers a drawing tool for you to doodle your thoughts.

2. Depending on what device you are using, the documents that you skitch on is turned to a PDF file by Evernote. Once you are done with the doodles, you can save it back to a PDF and have it preserved in your Evernote account.

3. You can use it to take notes and you have the freedom to write whatever you want on whatever document you have. It helps you improve your productivity by marking up exact parts of a certain document.

4. How is this helpful?

a. If you have a blog that focuses on a particular service, you can use skitch to specifically display what you are talking about. It is hard to engage with customers via the Internet, but with images, they will be better understood.

b. The best part is if you have already altered a certain document through skitch, it will be connected to Evernote where your blog is situated. This is just the perfect way to keep everything in one place and help you get things done at a quicker pace.

c. When you have used the Evernote feature of Clipwebsites, you will basically have a screenshot version of that article. How about if you have taken a photo of something that has privacy written all over it? Good question. Skitch can take care of it. With a blur option, it can keep security information classified.

4. Email Blog Post Ideas

Adults and students have at least used emails once in their life. Some have more than others depending on their networks and purpose. The technology that is the email has a universal appeal and have been used by people around the globe. Some may say that it is one of the most basic skills required in relation to the usage of technology. So why not go back to the basics? You can send blog post ideas from your email to Evernote. This is what you should do:

1. Go to your Evernote email address and search for the button that says "Account Info" then you will need to go and click "More Account Settings".

2. You can make sure that whatever idea you have, it is placed in the specific notebook and tag to make it easier to locate in the future. You can save your ideas through this format created by Michael Hyatt: Note Name @Notebook Name #Tag Name !YYYY/MM/DD.

3. Once you have done that, you are cleared to send you email. Make sure you use the naming system correctly; otherwise it would end up in your default folder. It isn't something to worry about, but would save a lot of time and it wouldn't be a hassle.

The basic need for this is that once you receive an email regarding something you are interested to put inside your blog or use as reference, you can immediately link that certain idea to you Evernote account without having to do a lot of different things. This will allow you to forward that email for you to check out later, it will definitely save time and energy.

Some people have the tendency to check their email and find something that they deem worthy to add to their blogs. But since what you want to do is in your head, it would probably be forgotten the more you flick through your email. By emailing your blog post ideas, you won't need to worry about leaving your current application to go to Evernote to save your idea then come back to your email.

5. Keeping Track Of Progress

How do you keep up with your progress? If you want to successfully create a blog that would cater to the needs of people around the world, you need to make sure that whatever you are doing, it is going in the right direction. By keeping track of your progress, you can determine if your current technique is helping or should you tweak it to get the optimum result.

How is Evernote related to all these marketing strategies? There are actually a lot of ways that Evernote is playing a significant role in promoting and organizing your blog. Evernote helps track the goals that you are pursuing by letting you create a specific notebook with weekly current notes to see where you are up to so far.

1. CoSchedule can be used to determine the social media shares your blog is currently reeling in. By deciding how much these numbers are, it would also identify the amount of people that have access to your blog and how much views it is getting.

2. Evernote is linked with the Google Analytics tool to survey the amount of traffic your blog is getting. Of course, the more traffic there is, the more people have access to the blog. In the best case scenario, you will need to make sure that your blog has the ability to keep up with the increasing amount of traffic.

3. Emailing subscribers through Campaign Monitor and KISSmetrics is a technique to catch the attention of the people that have already subscribed to your blog. Perhaps they have forgotten to check out your latest blog posts or forgot the means to access it, this will help them link themselves with your site and engage in the activities that you can offer.

4. Customer conversions through Intercom and KISSmetrics also need to be increased to ensure that your blogs are heading in the right direction.

Naturally, you will need to alter the way you go about creating and marketing your website based on your track records every week. Evernote will help you track your progress to see how your blog fares with the various sites online.

6. Blog Posting Directly From Evernote

Evernote has already proven to be force to be reckoned with in the world of productivity apps and essential organizational guides. Evernote is constantly improving and innovating its standards to meet the growing demand of technology driven people. Since people have used Evernote mainly to keep important documents online, as well as use it is a medium for note taking and presenting, it is a great pleasure to know that Evernote can be used to post blogs directly.

This save people the hassle of transferring and translating pieces of blog ideas into different mediums to have the end result. It has been understood by people in the past, but it can be tedious and a waste of time. Plus with more mediums involved with your blog post, some information may have been disregarded and lost, not to mention have it saved it completely different apps.

Sold with the idea? This is how you can achieve this:

1. Create a blog with the application called Postach.io. This is a reliable Evernote partner that when linked, can post specific details written on Evernote to your blog. All you need to do at this point is create a new account, if you haven't done so already, and write your email address with your preferred password.

2. As soon as that is complete, link Postach.io with your Evernote account, which can be found in your new blog.

3. To use the blog properly, you will need to identify a blog name that fits you and that fits what you will have as the content of your blog. You will also have to make a domain and customize your URL suitable for your liking.

4. The next part, you don't really need to do. Postach.io is programmed to make a notebook within your Evernote account. Don't worry; although this isn't optional, this is vital to post anything on Evernote to your blog.

5. If you have a blog post that is ready to be posted online, tag that note as "Published". This will then post whatever your note is into your blog online. It's pretty once you get the hang of it.

7. Post To Wordpress From Evernote

Wordpress has become one of the most used blogging websites in the world to date and growing by the minute. The fact that it is free to set up and has an option to maintain a free and openly viewed website is appealing to many. Not to mention that it is simple to use and once you get the hang of it, you will completely adore the results it produces. Wordpress is dynamic too, trying to make it easier for people to blog. But it would need the capabilities of Evernote to improve its utilization.

Why not mix one of the biggest blogging sites to one of the most popular productivity apps? It is completely achievable! Although Postach.io is a blog website that is primarily for Evernote users, it may be a hassle for people who have a successful blogging life using Wordpress. Converting one blog to another is a complete waste of time and something has been done about it. This is how it works:

1. Before starting anything, you need to grasp what an IFTTT service is. It is basically something that connects you to other services. IFTTT with Wordpress?

2. All you need to do is activate the channel and use a trigger or an action to post whatever you want on your Wordpress blog. IFTTT links Wordpress and Evernote together in a way that whatever triggers you generate in one, it would have a consequential effect in the other.

3. You can even link whatever tags you have on Evernote on whatever tags you have on Wordpress. The best way is to archive all your blog posts and once it's created in a note, you can create the action that leads it to your Wordpress account.

4. By adding recipes to the Wordpress and Evernote, it can easily allow you to post on Wordpress whatever you have written on Evernote. By using a trigger, action and ingredient, you don't need to manually post blogs on Wordpress, rather have one application do everything for you. Ingredients are made of specific pieces of data that is created in the light of whatever trigger you decided to have. IFTTT makes this happen.

8. More Tips For Bloggers

All in all, Evernote is the right mix of productive creativity and disciplined task allocating and accomplishments. The following are just a summary of the features that Evernote manifests that helps bloggers and also a few additional tips that will further guarantee that Evernote is a great investment.

- The feature that allows me to clip parts of websites makes it a blogger's dream come true. By screenshotting ideas and concepts that inspire you, this will make it more efficient for you to store those inspirations without going through the hassle of going through various websites.

- Need to communicate with other people regarding your blog? You can use the in-built Evernote chat program that makes everything accessible all in one app. This will also save your device memory having to keep track of your diverse applications.

- A productivity app wouldn't be an efficient productivity app without the help of reminders. Evernote keeps you informed on the upcoming events and helps you focus on what needs to be done. Evernote not only reminds you of the dates, it would include the details of that reminder together with its information.

- Large projects often frighten people. The immense workload that goes towards its success can sometimes be overwhelming. With Evernote, you can manage it better by segregating it into workable chunks of responsibilities. Before you know it, you'll be able to complete your checklist in time for the blog project deadlines.

- Although we are moving towards a more technologically advanced society, some of us can't help but to write notes down with pen and paper than typing it all out. The freedom to write your thoughts freely is a preferred choice. How can you save your ideas on paper without wasting time having to type it all out? Use the scanning method on Evernote. This is excellent when collating all your different handwritten notes for you to use later on with blog ideas.

• Speaking of blog ideas, there is the template feature that Evernote has developed. For blog writing, you can make a blog post idea template that you can copy and paste for you to use as a guide. Having several blog idea notes at once, you can savor every single idea that you might forget otherwise.

Chapter 6:
Random Uses For Evernote that just might make your day

More General Tips

Need more help with how Evernote could be useful to you? Because, there are numerous other ways that Evernote could be used for your liking.

Here are the five different ways where Evernote may deem useful for your use. You may even be surprised by what it can do:

01. Storing your Medical Records

Placing all of your personal and family doctor's names, contact information and addresses could serve useful to you. Especially for someone who has been previous been admitted before or is required to see the doctor regularly.

02. Recording License Plates

When in your repair car shop or if you are trying to sell your car to a client and they ask for your plate number or car information. Have no fear, take photos of what your car looks like including its license plate to avoid having to go back home just to gain the information.

03. Best Haircut

Say goodbye to bad haircuts. The rare times you get a great haircut, you tend to want to take photos of how it looks and how proud of how sexy you look. Why not keep that haircut photo to show to your next barber visit? He will definitely know what you mean when you explain what haircut you want to achieve.

04. Interesting Webpages

There are numerous articles, may it be on facebook or 9gag, that contains interesting information we may want to read. Although, the problem is, we may not have the time at the moment to be able to read it or we're already reading another article. Simply save the webpage with the use of the Evernote Web Clipper extension and be able to read it another time.

05. Travel Packing List

This is what a lot of travelers need. There are numerous times that individuals may experience going to travel to another location, when realizing that they don't have everything they need. It sucks the most especially when it's travelling to another country. Be sure to write down what you packed the next time you travel; it could serve as a list where you can checklist if you have all the items that you brought to the trip to bring at home.

Evernote for Writing – Get more done with distraction free writing using Evernote

This goes out to all those professional and amateur writers out there. Evernote could apply to your writing needs. May it be for a school article, a novel or just a quick speech, Evernote provides a distraction free writing environment for all.

Here are the six tips on how to maximize the use of Evernote when writing:

01. Writing for Perfection

End your distracted days by applying the full-screen feature when you partake in your writing. The ample white spice around your work provides the perfect boost for your productivity. When applying full-screen, it is the perfect way to write down any of your notes, ideas and your full on articles without distraction

02. Viewpoint Control

Apart from the provided effect of full-screen. Evernote has the ability to provide a dual screen effect. Where on the left could contain your notes, notebooks, shortcuts and tags, while the right side of your screen is where your current note resides. Stay in topic of what is required for you to write with this nifty feature.

03. Format

As you focus on writing, highlight selected text in or to provide for you the alternative to format your copy. All you need to do is click to change the font, size and style of those specific words.

04. Categorize and Tag Swiftly

Be able to categorize your note without the hassle of having to leave your writing environment. As seen on the page there is an icon called '*Daily knowledge*', add your tags on the box next to it!

05. Photos to Boost Creativity

A picture may be worth a thousand words, but you can't rely on it to finish your book. However, you could use it in order to help boost creativity and provide you with some support in terms of creating a visual narrative for the writer's pleasure. Drag photos into your writing space or click on the paperclip icon in the menu to add photos.

06. Search

The best thing about Evernote, is the ability to comprehensively and swiftly search for the content you need.

Evernote for Songwriters – Capture Ideas, Write Lyrics and Save Drafts all from Evernote

For those who are into the music industry or may be close to someone who is a songwriter. It is obvious to tell the struggle that artists take in order to create masterful songs that would capture their audience the way they anticipate to.

What songwriters have to overcome is the resistance to start as well as the resistance to finish, which includes applying your ideas as they come. Usually, when you gain a boost of creativity, you don't have your guitar on you and you may have to wait until tomorrow, but what happens is that the creativity tends to leave by that time.

So, here are the tips to change your musical life and how to use it to your advantage:

● **Recording Any Audio**

This could be best when you have a stroke of luck in terms of the melody or the sound that you want your song to be like. This usually works for those who have a computer. There will be a microphone icon placed within Evernote where you can record what ever it is you need to record.

● **Writing Your Lyrics**

What artists may want to do, is once there is a melody in mind, they start to write the lyrics to the song they want to achieve. This way, when you revisit your audio note the following day, the lyric ideas have been remembered. What this achieves is the ability for writers to free up their creative mind than trying to remember any lyrics.

● **Share The Talent**

Singers may want to consider gaining feedback from their musical peers and see what they think of the upcoming hit that you would be creating. Or, the use of collaborating with artists could become easily done with the feature of sharing that Evernote has.

Rather than having to e-mail it back and forth from artist to artist, speed up your writing process by clicking the share button to share your work with your co-writer or peers.

The application to boost your singing career is here! Make the most of this advantage while you can.

Keeping Focused – Don't let distractions throw you off focus.

This could be in relation to staying focus while writing. People who attempt to try out their managerial skills or those who naturally love to manage their time may tend to get thrown off by distractions and forgetting what it is they had to do.

Everyone has gone through the distraction phase. This could be the school girl trying to finish her report paper for class the next day using Evernote, while being on YouTube watching monkeys dance or the business man who is meant to provide a presentation to their work the next day, but ends up scrolling through the depths of their Facebook page. It isn't a shame to admit that you may have experienced this, everyone has.

If you think about it this way, apart from some people having the will to finish studying or doing their tasks, the environment plays a huge role in your ability to focus on your work. For example: if the TV is on as you work, you may overhear what is showing and end up watching a show for an hour when you should be finishing your work. If that TV was to be turned off, there would be less distractions for you to create an excuse.

Evernote solves this problem with the use of the full-screen feature, but how else do they decrease the urge to procrastinate?

Well, what you could do, is create a '*Distraction to-do list*' for yourself.

What is this you ask? It is a to-do list for all the things you wanted to search or look up on as you were working. Don't get it? Think about it this way, you may be writing an article that needs to be passed by the end of the day. During the time you try to accomplish this task, you randomly remember the time your mum has told you to cook dinner for the next day and seeing as it is important to you, you are attempted to search up recipes right then and there instead of doing work.

To avoid that distraction, place it in your '*Distraction to-do list*' and once you are done with your work, you could go back to achieve what it is you wanted to achieve that has nothing to do with your writing.

Evernote Shortcuts

Did you know that Evernote could be driven entirely by the use of your keyboard? No? Well now you do! But, what are these shortcuts that you should be warned about?

Provided below are the numerous ways you could use shortcuts to use Evernote on your desktop:

Evernote For Mac Shortcuts

Create notes and notebooks

⌘ N	Create a new note
^ ⌘ ⇧ N	Open a new note window
⌘ ⇧ N	Create a new notebook
^ ⌘ N	Create a new note, audio note, or screenshot with Quick Note

Collect everything

Clip full screen	Start screen capture mode. Aditionally, check out our Web Clipper.
Control + Alt + V	Paste the contents from your Mac Clipboard as a new note
Drag files to Evernote	Drag and drop a selected file onto the Evernote menu bar to add it as a note in Evernote.

Write and edit efficiently

⇧ ⌘ V	Paste as plain text
^ ⌘ T	Create a new tag
⌘ :	Show spelling
⌘ ;	Check spelling and grammar
⇧ ⌘ T	Insert a to-do checkbox
⇧ ⌘ L	Insert a table
⇧ ⌘ H	Insert a horizontal line
⌘ K	Add a hyperlink
⇧ ⌘ K	Remove a hyperlink
⇧ ⌘ M	Merge notes
^ ⌘ M	Choose a notebook for a selected note

Find anything

^ ⌘ E	Search in Evernote
⌘ J	Search your notebooks
⌘ F	Search within a note
⌥ ⌘ F	Search your notes
⌥ ⌘ 1	Access your notes
⌥ ⌘ 2	Access all of your notebooks
⌥ ⌘ 4	Go to Atlas view
⇧ ⌘ I	Show or hide note information — this includes title, tags, location, and time and date the note was created or updated.
⌘ Q	Quit Evernote (only temporarily, of course)

Evernote For Windows Shortcuts

Create notes and notebooks

Ctrl + N	Create a new note
Ctrl + Shift + N	Create a new notebook
Collect everything	
Win + PrintScreen	Start screen capture mode. Aditionally, check out our Web Clipper
Control + Alt + V	Paste the contents from your clipboard as a new note

Write and edit efficiently

Ctrl + Shift + V	Paste from clipboard with unformatted text
Ctrl + V	Paste from clipboard with original formatting
Ctrl + Shift + T	Create a new tag
F7	Check spelling
Ctrl + Shift + C	Insert a to-do checkbox
Ctrl + Shift +-	Insert a line break in a paragraph
Ctrl + E	Center text
Ctrl + Shift + B	Create a bulleted list
Ctrl + Shift + O	Create a numbered list
Ctrl + K	Add a hyperlink
Ctrl + Shift + R	Remove a hyperlink

Find anything

Ctrl + shift + S	Create a new saved search
Ctrl + Shift + A	Reset search
Win + Shift + F	Find in Evernote
F2	Rename saved search
F6	Start search and move to first highlighted keyword
Ctrl + Q	Quit Evernote (only temporarily, of course)

Chapter 7:
Travel Hacking with Evernote

1. General Travel Tips

You have planned your trip for nearly a month now before school ends, compiling numerous articles on information about your destination for vacation, the best places to go and number one places to be.

But, what would be most unfortunate is when you end up going to the trip, you can't bring your heavy laptop around with all the information you need being a tourist. Why not use your handy-dandy smart device and use your Evernote application to access all the information you need.

Not convinced how Evernote could help you during your travel? Well, here are some tips on how to tackle your next travel with the use of Evernote:

• **Get City Smart**

Learn to organize your notes into different folders for each city that you are expected to visit on your vacation. So, information on the different hotels, restaurants and other tourist destinations that you could visit will be within a touch of a button.

• Evernote to Check In

If ever your hotel has requested to see your reservation receipt, having Evernote on you could deem easy when you are able to showcase your reservations to the receptionist. However, if you don't know where you are and you can show the taxicab the location you need to go to.

• Share the Experience

When using your smart device to capture your memories while travelling abroad, taking photos of all the food, the restaurants and the people you meet. You can share these experiences with your friend with the share feature that Evernote possesses. If ever your friend or families were planning to go to the destination where you have been to in the past, then simply sharing where you have gone and your experience would help a lot when shared to others.

• Going Global

When travelling abroad it can seem hard to get Wi-Fi connection to access the notes you saved for your trip. Becoming a premium user of Evernote allows you to access your notes even when you are offline. Just be sure that you have synced your devices before the plane has taken off.

2. Be spontaneous, but plan your trip

Before going on any trip, whether it is for business or for vacation, you need to plan your itinerary well in order to make for a productive trip. What people would usually need is numerous pieces of paper to track down your schedule and different platforms to search just to be able to keep in track of how your day would go.

With Evernote, you can plan your trip all in one platform, from your flight details to where your hotel is located. This will end up being convenient for you, especially those who will travel to locations they have never been before.

Here are tips on how to plan your trip well with the use of Evernote:

• Plan Wherever and Whenever

Make sure that if you have Evernote in one device that you have it in all your other devices. This would serve convenient when you want to plan your trips, you could access any device closes to you in order to capture the information you need to keep and inspiration you come across.

• Packing List

Ever get that feeling that you are forgetting something once you have left your house to go on a trip? Well, worry no more. Use Evernote as your packing list. Place all the items that you are bringing with you in lists under one note in order to keep organized and easy access to what it is you have and what it is you need to pack when the situation arises.

- Clipping Away

Clip information on websites as you come across them. For example, you find yourself reading an article that says: 'Top Ten Places to Visit in the Philippines' and travel in mind, it sounds like a decent place to visit so clip the page and save this file into your Travel notebook on Evernote. Just tag the destinations that is included, you can even consider placing itineraries or tips that your favorite travel bloggers suggests.

- Travelling with Other People

When planning a trip with more than one person, sharing Evernote to your peers could be very useful. What usually happens is people get too busy to meet up to constantly plan, but if there were a device that would connect everyone together it would be convenient.

3. Collect Travel Ideas

Evernote is not specifically an application for travellers; it is actually what I like to call a *'Chameleon'* application that is generalized for everyone. From business people to students to travelers, but this is an application that could seem to be born for the use of travellers.

When planning trips, you don't necessarily have to have a definite plan of what you are going to do. But, you could have an outline plan of what you are going to do. In our world of technology today we are constantly bombarded with numerous articles from people around the world through Facebook, Twitter or any other social media sites. Giving us ideas on how we would like to spend our travelling or vacation days.

Even with all these articles, you may forget what it is that you have read a few days after reading it. It could become a pain when you are trying to show your parents or friends what you want to do when you travel.

Keep all your travelling ideas into Evernote, clipping articles and taking pictures of what you have seen people doing during their vacation time to give you an idea of how you want to spend your vacation.

- **Remembering Location Ideas**

Let's say your friend had just got back from their vacation and is telling you about numerous places they have been to, as you try to search up that location, they start talking about another location

In order to keep the location idea with you, just find a location on Google Maps, tap the Info Card for the place, then right click the search box that takes you to a screen where you can share it to Evernote for storing.

• Storing Written Notes

If ever your friend recommends you a place to visit and hands you a napkin of where that place is, just capture it with your phone and place it onto your Evernote notebook for your travel ideas. This will prevent you from having to keep so many pieces of paper from what other friends have suggested and you could access this information whenever you want with Evernote.

4. Create A Travel Checklist

Checklists could serve as a galore for everyone's daily lives, may it be for those business men who need to note down what they need to do when assigned a task or for traveller's who need a checklist for packing.

In this section, checklists are traveller's best friends. Usually, you would think a checklist is only used to tick down your packing inventory so that you don't forget whatever it is you need to bring. However, even if that is greatly helpful to travellers, you could use checklists for numerous other reasons when you travel.

Here are the numerous ways you could use checklists for when you travel:

• Packing Inventory

Of course, there is always the problem of forgetting items when you leave. Some people even tend to forget their passports during their rush to get to the airport. Imagine having to go back home just to get it with the worry of missing your flight. With a checklist ready of what you need to bring for your up coming travel, you won't ever have to forget your items again! Just tick what you have and pack what you haven't yet.

The packing inventory checklist could also be used when packing your items when you're coming back home. What would be most unfortunate if you end up leaving something important in another country, so use it to be able to keep all your items before you come back home to prevent forgetting anything

- Places to Go, People to See

You may not have a complete inventory of what you will do where you are going, but what is also good to consider is placing a couple of places that you are keen on seeing when you travel.

For example, using a checklist when you go to Vietnam to remember to visit the War Museum or the Cu Chi Tunnels or even locations your friends have suggested for you to visit. It may provide for you an idea on what you can do when you travel, which could serve convenient when you visit locations you have never been before.

5. Use It For World Travel

You may want to travel within your country, but for those who have planned to travel to a completely different territory, using Evernote could be your new best friend.

Here is how Evernote could be helpful for you when you want to take the world by storm:

- Scanning Your Passport

It is obvious to everyone that you need your passport with you when you travel abroad. Those applying for a visa may be required to present a copy of their recent passport document. Usually people would have to photocopy their passport countless times because you may have forgotten where you placed the photocopied file or even the digital file for printing.

Imagine only having to scan your passport every time you have a new passport, if your current passport is scanned into Evernote, you can use it any and every time it is required of you.

- Travel Goat Settings

Everyone loves to have an idea of where they want to travel to in life, some may have countless destinations and others may just have a few. Regardless, it is convenient to have your travels dreams in one location waiting to be explored.

You could write down in a new note on Evernote the location and everything about that location in order for you to be ready. Having photos of the location could serve as inspiration for you to be motivated to get to that destination as your travel goals.

● Business Development During World Travel

If ever your job requires you to travel a lot around the world and you are required to develop projects during these trips. Well, Evernote can be easily accessed as you travel along. This could be while you're in the plane or even casually hanging out in your hotel.

Take out your Evernote application from either one of your devices, whether it is your laptop or smart phones while on your travels to be able to capture what it is you seem is appropriate and in relation to your business project. This will end up providing a lot of productivity when show casing your project to your boss at the end of your trip.

6. Documenting Your Trip

One of the reasons we have smart devices with a camera already installed is to be able to capture our memories as we go along in life. This is the same for when we travel, everyone is constantly taking photos of different things that they find interesting.

What Evernote helps provide is to keep all your memories and experiences in one area for when you document your trip, this can be both used for those aspiring bloggers or travellers alike

● Evernote for Bloggers

Bloggers who go on vacation usually have a system of how they would write down experiences for the up coming blog. But, usually, even for experienced bloggers as the trip goes down the line, it becomes evident that it is hard to keep track of everything and anything you see.

Using the camera on your smart device, bloggers could simply snap everything they want to mention on their blog from what they see on the street to what is provided in their restaurants and keep all the information in a notebook for when they get back from the trip.

This provides more time to enjoy and look around than jotting down all the experiences that could get lost as the trip goes.

- Evernote for Travellers

Even if you aren't an aspiring blogger, you could still snap your experiences down in your notes within Evernote as something to look back to once the trip is over. These stocked up information could also be used when talking to relatives and friends about your trip and telling them how it was. Another thing that this information could be used for is when you want to share information to your peers who would be planning to go on the same trip as you.

- Evernote Food and Evernote Hello

Both Evernote Food and Evernote Hello are applications you could add in addition to your original Evernote application.

Evernote Food is for those foodies who want to experience different restaurants when they travel. It allows you to search for these restaurants and to create a list of places you would want to visit.

Evernote Hello allows you to gather contact information, photos and location information about every person that you have met during your travels

7. Travelling Assistant

When travelling, it is usually expected for you to be able to soak in your new experiences including the sights, sounds and the food that you consume. To have the capability to open your mind, allowing yourself in these new perspectives of life and the new flavors that you take in from the different cultures and cuisines.

However, some people end up not being in the moment of their travels because there is just so much to deal with while you're on the road and away from the usual.

Here are some ways you could create Evernote to revolve around being your best travel assistant to free yourself from the shackles of being responsible for keeping all your requirements from your trip and actually enjoy the vacation:

- Consider Going 'Paperless'

Imagine all the documents that you would need to carry on your next trip, so many papers you would have to keep track of in order to fly. Typically, what people would have to deal with when travelling is booking confirmations, hotel confirmations, boarding passes, maps, event tickets or conference passes imagine keeping all those on paper.

The thing is, Evernote comes with a forwarding email address where users are allowed to forward their emails to. It can be synced through all devices and confirmation emails could be sent to be able to bring all the requirements on your smart device wherever you go.

- Tracking Expense

Not everyone is keen on knowing what they spend during their trips, but for those who do like to know where their money goes. Use Evernote to keep track of your daily expenses. This can be achieved simply by taking a picture of receipts as you travel and keeping them in one notebook collection in order to refer back to it.

You are also able to take pictures of the menus you have come across to remember the meals you tried on your journey. Or, better yet, as you take these notes on your device, Evernote is able to keep track of the locations of your restaurant by viewing your notes in Atlas View.

8. Keep a Traveller's Diary

It is a living need among traveller's in order to capture what is out of the norm. For example, being from the United States and seeing how different living is like in countries within Asia.

Technology has changed the way travellers would usually take down their notes. From having to write down on a piece of paper to just tapping down your notes in your device. You could jot down something on your smart device faster than you would write, placing your ideas in hopes that it would transpire into your next travel piece.

But, it doesn't give you the same feel when typing in your smart phone than it would to write down on your very own journal.

Introducing Moleskine

Evernote has collaborated with Moleskine who is famous for their creative and popular notebooks that the cool kids have. The combination has provided the old feel of how a written notebook would be like with the new digital and searchable copy.

It is simply really, write your notes and draw your picture the way you would normally like to when you write in a notebook. Snap photos using the 'Page Camera' and Evernote will be able to digitalize it for you, INCLUDING making the text that you have searchable.

Once saved up in your device and synced with all your other Evernote applications on your smart device and laptop, you will be able to keep track of all the notes you have written down as you travel on your different devices.

There is even the ability to take a step further and including 'Smart Stickers' that can be placed on your writing in order to associate with your own searchable tags.

As a traveller, being able to keep your writing ideas somewhere that could be easily accessed is convenient. It would end up being a complete hassle, while having to take out your notebook in the middle of a busy street because you have an idea to write about. Using Evernote would just have you to take out your smart device and jot down it quickly and swiftly.

9. Business Travel Helper

If you are a businessman, you could see Evernote as your little portable office.

Here are five ways that Evernote could be used for business:

01. Conference Contacts

If ever you happen to be at a conference, you could use Evernote to snap the new people you meet (preferably wearing their name tags clearly on their clothing) and to snap the new business cards that you have received from clients or prospects, so that it could be later searched.

This means that you can tag the conference you both attended in order to be able to get the name of the client or prospect that you have made contact with. Before conferences, it is convenient to take a look at your previous conference contacts to refresh your mind of who you met and where.

02. Business Skype Conversations

When using Skype to contact your colleagues, you could use the Callnote Application on top of your Evernote Application. What Callnote does is that it notifies the other party that they are being recorded as the call begins. The whole recording is then placed directly into Evernote either after you have finished the call or once you have been able to review it.

03. Long-Distance Business Collaborations

If ever you have to collaborate with a business partner from across the globe, simply sharing your documents with them will make your collaboration so much more easier instead of having to fly in and out constantly. You could lessen your 20 different trips to 5 ones to save time and money for future collaborations and when necessary.

04. Sending in Expense Reports

When the time has come for you to send your boss the expenses you have consumed while on a business trip. You can consider reducing paper usage by taking a picture of your receipts into a note, then adding a spreadsheet to create your summary. The note could then be shared or directly emailed to your boss for further review.

05. Working on the Travel

Before going on your business trip, make sure you create offline notes that you could review and sync up your devices so the information such as to-do lists, important documents and more could be easily accessed.

Get productive even on the road!

10. Never Carry Receipts Again While Travelling

Here's a scenario that people tend to experience usually when travelling for business:

You are required to meet with a client as you are on the road and you have just paid $100 for a meal for two at a fancy restaurant. You need to keep the receipt just for your business' expense and tax purposes. You quickly write down the meeting details behind the receipt and place it in your pocket.

Easy right?

Well, at the end of the day as you empty your pockets it doesn't seem to be anywhere, when you realize it has fallen out of your pocket as you were walking or while you were getting change for the store.

Without the receipt, there's no reimbursement, no deduction, no nothing. You have no proof that you have paid for a meal in the name of the business. Although, now there is an easier way to keep all your receipts in order to make sure you get your expense summary report in on time.

So, here's what you will need in order to stop carrying your receipts during business trips:

01. Evernote – To be able to store photos of your receipts and place all your notes within one area for your convenience.

02. Expensify – This is an application that allows you to create expense reports with ease with its online software. The best thing about this is that it's free!

03. Smart Device – A lot of people have smart devices in the modern day, even your local storeowner has it. Although, the first two services don't require a smart device, but what having a smart device does is eliminate the use of having receipts on you where you go!

04. Receipt

With all these combined, you just need to take a picture of your receipts with the smart device you own, place it in Evernote so that it is documented for when you use expensify in creating your expense reports. You could even throw away your receipt once you have taken a photo and create your expense report after since; after all, you have scanned it onto your Evernote application.

Chapter 8:
Evernote for Programmers

1) Programmer's Notebook

Programmers will understand that management is key to any success. Programmers initially create codes that computers will be able to comprehend and function itself to work towards that goal. Programmers could be experts of designing, testing, fixing or writing a certain code for programs. This would in turn manipulate codes to customize them to get a required behavior. You don't have to be a licensed programmer to get the credentials; anyone with certain basic points will comprehend its purpose. However, it can be illegal in some areas to market your programming skills without prior legitimate training.

Whether you are an amateur or professional programmer, you will need a place to store codes so you can come back later and use. Programmers need that type of application. Programming requires technique and skill. Imagine having to experiment on a specific sequence of programming codes and you have nowhere to keep a memory of it. Evernote has got you covered.

How can Evernote benefit programmers?

1. Evernote has a feature to look back at notes with particular codes that you've arranged to get a specific outcome. Perhaps codes to digitally alter game plays and mechanics. By labeling those notes for the codes, you can immediately track down the note you need.

2. In relation to the previous point, you will need to organize these notes into topics and their subtopics. If you're an avid programmer, it is safe to say that you will be exposed to various codes. By marking these codes into notes, you will be able to segregate codes for designing, for instance, and then have a subcategory for web design.

3. Have something you need to save in a website? Don't go through the hassle of encoding every random code. Although programmers create and read codes as if it were as simple as writing down letters from the alphabet, it gets tiring and requires a lot of effort. By using web clip, saving these codes is a piece of cake and will be a better way to look back and use.

4. To top it all off: the application is absolutely free. If you're curious to see what Evernote can do to make your programming life more productive then just download it and create an account. You'll find it beneficial, not only to your programming needs, but with everything else.

2) Code Snippets

Syntax highlighting and formatting are what programmers normally use. Some may not trust Evernote to have the capability to cater to syntax highlighting and formatting resulting in pursuing other apps that cater to this. There have been instances where copying and putting codes on Evernote loses the value of syntax highlights and formatting. But with proper information and technique, you will be able to have a copy of an HTML posted in your Evernote account and have it pasted into other software. What you can try to do are some of these tips:

• First, you can try copying and pasting your code previews directly into Evernote via a markup.su/highlighter/ device. All you need to remember to do is to have your code placed into the box entitled "Source Code" and press the "Highlight" option. What it does it that it would then highlight the code with its preview that you can easily place on Evernote.

• If you don't prefer that kind of interface, you can always opt for another solution, which is to use a tool that would enable you to format a code and have the HTML that you need through hilite.me. This tool needs to be manually correct the Evernote notes code. Afterwards, you can put your HTML markup in any of the already created notes.

• Sometimes you would come across a simple and short code that you wouldn't be a bother typing out. Unlike other codes that goes on for miles, shorter codes can be web clipped and screenshot. You will then need to save it as a note and if you need it in the future, you can just type it out again.

- Some people would prefer a built in feature in Evernote that would allow code snippets. It is called "The Evernote Sublime plugin"; this can be taken to consideration when using SublimeTest 3. Otherwise, there is also the option of the characteristic called the "Markdown Editor for Evernote".

- There are other simpler options as already made markdown tools that would allow you to put down certain code snippets. This will enable you to then just copy the code.

3) Organize And Save Time

Evernote's purpose it to organize and save time in everything you do. By featuring characteristics of storing notes that can be easily searched and located, you won't have to physically storing everything on your walls, folders and desk. What better way to keep notes that are already out in the open by documenting it digitally?

There are people that are afraid to embark on a life that revolves around technology. Some have attested upgrading your life using the Internet as something difficult and complicated to use and comprehend. I mean, wouldn't you rather just go back to the basics? It's understandable that we still have those reservations and doubt. But you can't have a personal opinion without trying it out first.

There's a reason why millions of people have now resorted to applications to improve their lifestyle and productivity, with thousands more joining each day. Evernote has adapted to the needs of the people in a way that makes simple chores such as writing reminders down and memorizing notes. Remember that note you wrote at the back of a receipt safely tucked in your pocket? Yes, it is probably taking a swim in the washing machine about now. When you are enlightened by an idea, type it down in your Evernote account as a note. This syncs with your other devices and will be available for you to open up anywhere. It saves valuable time having to search for it and giving your brain a work out tracing back to the last place you've placed it.

You don't have to be someone who organizes their documents like a pro, you can just be an average Joe putting information on a web based platform. Just by starting off like that, you'll start to get a hang of it. Evernote allows you to tag your notes in a manageable manner. It keeps notebooks of different notes you've written for different projects and events. Tagging them to their specific relation will make it faster for you to get immediately (that is, if you've tagged them accordingly). Instead of going to your shelf to find a folder revolving around programming an application and looking up what you need in its alphabetical order, just go to the search bar on Evernote and retrieve whatever it is you're looking for.

Chapter 9:
Evernote for Sports

1.) Use Evernote To Write Down Drills And Warm Up Sequence

Sports and Evernote goes hand in hand perfectly. Although people would assume that sports is something that requires a more physical take, having the organization and planning capability that Evernote possesses makes it all the more valuable. You can't go straight into drills and warm up without the proper plan. You will end up not stretching and preparing the right muscles for the specific type of drills you want or you will find yourself doing the same drills that won't allow you to vary in progress.

Evernote can keep your drills and warm ups in notes under a specific folder. You can add and edit your drills on notes that you can mix and match based on what your goals are. For example, if you are preparing for a tennis tournament. Each training session has to be able to have drills that cover your major muscles and techniques. You can mix and match these drills and have and organized goal on what needs to be accomplished that day. However, your drills in preparation for a tournament aren't the same for drills to just improve your swing and speed off-season. It varies and with the guide of Evernote, it is feasible.

Don't forget to tag your drills and warm up trainings. Using the same tennis example, you will need to jot down the type of warm up methods that allow you to stretch and loosen up certain muscles. If you're focusing on your swing technique, you can search your tags related to the muscle in your arms so you can be assisted on what you need to focus on. Preventing muscle strain and injuries is significant in sports whether playing as an amateur or professional. One slight injury can keep you benched for the rest of your life.

If you're the type of person to write and edit your drills and warm up ideas on paper, Evernote has taken that to account and made it easier to work with. By scanning and/or taking a photo of your doodles, you can keep it in store just in case you will need to check what exactly you will need to do on certain drills.

Evernote For Martial Arts

2.) Capture Techniques from YouTube

With tons of videos posted everyday and millions of viewers watching around 6 billion hours of video every month, YouTube has become one of the most popular video realms on the Internet today. There are deposits of various types of videos from DIYs, to news reports and music videos. One of the most trending types of videos would be self-help and tutorials. When it comes to sports and perfecting certain techniques, YouTube is a great way to improve your skill. Here are three ways Evernote plays a functional role of improving sport techniques:

- Evernote has the web clipper feature that would allow you to keep screen shots of physical actions that you can save. You can also preserve the URL for future look backs to trace where you've found it. This prevents repeated searches so you will be more efficient. The web clipper note only captures the techniques, but you will also be able to keep them in a system where you will be able to collage it.

- Since Evernote has designed the application detail that allows you to add your own notes to the web clips, you can look back in full precision certain tips on perfecting sports techniques. It is a simple and great way to teach you basic and skillful moves. It is one thing to have the captured images, but it is another to have your personal detailed description of each.

- To add, tags can be attached to those techniques to make it quicker to recall and reflect on. For example, if you prefer to improve your soccer kicks and tricks, you can web clip specific moves and note down reminders to yourself about your feet positioning and angle of the kicks. With more and more practice and with the helpful guidance of Evernote, reaching your goal would be painless to complete. To divide your soccer kicks and soccer tricks so as to not mix the notes, you can tag them to your own preference. For instance, (by using the "@" sign as the tagging mechanism on Evernote) you can have the @bicyclekick, @divingheader or the @scissorkick tags.

3.) Documents Seminars And Private Classes

Some people invest a lot of money on private classes, tutoring and group seminars and for a great purpose: to expand your learning to specific discussions and explore subject matter. Documenting and memorizing these discussions usually go unremembered and beyond recollection. Regardless of your brain memory capacity, you will just forget what you've learnt. Having Evernote kept at the ready, you won't need to stress about this much longer. What are the benefits of pursuing your sport targets with the guidance of Evernote?

• Classes in relation to sports don't always have to be in the comfort of the field, track, pool, etc. Sometimes, they have the instructions laid out in a classroom setting so personal note taking would be necessary. By handwriting your notes, you'll be able to quickly write down notes and scan them for review on Evernote. You can also have the option of taking a photo of your notes and file the image properly.

☐ However, if you have the preference of typing out every note, go ahead and create your note directly to the Evernote app.

• You can use Evernote on any electronic device as long as the application is downloaded. Your account can reach various gadgets, allowing you to write notes on your desktop computer and analyzing them on your smartphone. All you have to do is to sync all their notes so you won't have to worry about your location when it comes to writing and editing notes.

• How does this work? Your Evernote email address permits you to make adjustments to those notes from anywhere around the world. For instance, if you have a note dedicated to basketball rules, if there are up to date regulations that you need to brief yourself, will be able to do so.

• Not only can you share your notes on your sport seminars, you can have other people share theirs. You will be able to adjust your notes and discuss on certain topics. You can do this by making it public and importing them into other sharing methods such as Google Reader or Netvibes.

4.) Making Your Game Plan

If you are passionate about a sport, having a game plan is almost automatic and expected. Sports are just like any ordinary games; they need the strategy and organization to win the game. Having a game plan is something that is of the utmost importance and Evernote has got you covered.

Your sports game plans are supposed to be understood visually. However, by having long texts and paragraphs of how you want the game to be played specific isn't helpful at all. We have a sense of understanding when we see images in front of us. Game plans are more pictures and drawings than anything; your team will be able to comprehend these types of plans. By using the scanning method on your Evernote application or the image capture, you can get these ideas into an image for you to look at later. Evernote unfortunately hasn't developed game planning through a series of shapes and arrows yet, however this is the second best option.

Having a set of techniques that you can list and work on can also be done using Evernote. Your checklist keeps you focused on what you need to be doing in terms of preparation and organization whilst the reminder aspect refreshes your memory on things that has to be done. You won't forget to remind your team about the type of play the opponents are known for or the techniques that you can use to overcome their strengths. You can't expect to keep all these information in your head, by using Evernote it just eases your control in a more manageable way.

Every game plan towards an opponent differs from the rest. Each team has to be played with exact precision and system. You can't use a game plan that requires a defensive stance going against an also defensive team. By understanding your opponent's weaknesses and strengths, you need to be able to adapt your plan accordingly. If your opponent has great speed, but lacking control, use that to your advantage. By using a tag on each game plan, you can determine game plans you've used before and alter it to fit your new opponents.

Evernote For Soccer Players

5.) Storing Soccer Videos

Soccer is one of the most well known sports in the world. With just a soccer ball in your arson, you can play soccer individually or with a team in any environment in the world. Many amateur soccer players or budding soccer enthusiasts always look for ways to improve their skill and technique by keeping up to date on the latest improvements on soccer equipment and direction. Even if you're not aiming to be the next Lionel Messi or Cristiano Ronaldo, playing the sport for fun also requires research and experimentation.

YouTube has been the source of plenty of tutorials due to its free and easily accessible nature. How can Evernote assist any soccer lessons? Evernote has the ability to web clip certain URLs that make it easier for videos to be located and played. These instructional videos will then enable users to look back and use it to their advantage. It doesn't only mean to keep track of one certain video; soccer videos can be web clipped plenty at a time.

By using the web clipper, you can add notes on what you need to improve based on the soccer videos and what you can take from it. This is more of a self-taught technique that you can consider doing. The good thing about videos is that it gives a visual aspect of learning that makes it easier to understand. Evernote has taken this to account when perfecting a skill and performance so the web clipper feature is completely useful in this regard.

For someone who has an extensive background on soccer instructional videos, it will be hard to locate them individually. Since there thousands of soccer instructional videos readily available online, you won't be able to remember each video entirely. Keeping an organized filing system on Evernote through applicable tags and references, you can look back at the URLs and your notes with ease. What makes Evernote a great application is that it keeps storing soccer videos uncomplicated. Young adults will be able to use the application trouble-free to improve their game and adults may use it for themselves or to guide younger children.

6.) Web Clipper For Soccer Articles & Guides

Web clipper only isn't used for storing and keeping track of soccer instructional videos, you can use web clipper for soccer articles and guides. Soccer is a dynamic sport and having reports on the latest soccer news and tricks will make it easier to keep up with the global soccer movement. There are plenty of soccer players that have the skill and technique that you idolize and by using Evernote, you'll be able to collate this equipped with the proper guides to make it better for you to duplicate and execute.

Having Evernote in the ready, the web clipper feature can track down individual guides and rules on how to play the game based on what your personal capabilities. You can screenshot these guides and put them next together with the different guides found online. Not only can you use it for current guides, you can use it to look back on some samples that you've found before. The whole reason for Evernote's existence when it comes to soccer-related documents is the easy filing storage. With the searching method, you can look back on the URLs that you've saved on the soccer articles you love to keep and the guides that you have completed or still need to complete.

You can find thousands of guides for your disposal on the Internet. The best thing about it is that Evernote can keep plenty at a time. Don't forget to tag your articles and guides to make it useful in the future. When it comes to soccer articles and guides, you can use tags and notebooks that are specific to each category. For example, you can have ones that are primarily for the different leagues from different countries. Or you have ones that are focusing on guides from different positions.

Web clipping has the best features when screen shooting certain parts of your soccer interests. By having the actual image of the guides, you will have a better understanding on what they are requiring you to do and which parts of the body you should focus on.

Evernote For Cycling

7.) Keep Your Bike's Stats

A biker's bike is their most treasured item. Well of course, you wouldn't be a biker without one. Your bike's dimensions should be properly stored and kept for you to be able to look back in the future. There are plenty of times where people forget their measurements and it would take them a while to memorize and measure again. By keeping the dimensions safe and sound on your Evernote, you can access it almost anywhere.

By storing your bike's dimensions, you will be able to have the right information just in case you need it. Sometimes people disregard this about their bicycles but it would help in the long run. For example when you go travelling to another place, having the bike handles and storage room in your vehicle can only be done if you know how large your bike is. Proper preparation is needed when situations like this arise. Another example would be if your current bike is broken and you need some parts to be replaced or you need a new bike that needs to have the same measurements, you could get another one with your exact desires.

All you need to do is to store the measurements as notes on Evernote. Furthermore, you can store the serial number of your bicycle. You don't have to type each one down, although if you prefer to do so then go ahead, you can always just take a photo of the number and keep it ready. You can also keep a copy of the serial numbers of your other bike gears. Who knows, you might need it someday.

You can also send all these measurements and serial numbers to a friend or another person. Don't forget that the Evernote email address allows for this to happen. If you need something fixed or get a bike similar to yours, you can just send the information any time you want without having to measure it all one by one and then send it. Have it stored safely in corresponding notebooks and notes to make it easier for you to look back and locate.

8.) Capture Races And Events

As a cyclist, you would want to keep a copy of your races as well as have a close notice on your future events. Cyclists usually only have one event that they have been training hard for. Unlike soccer and basketball players where there are constant games to be played year round, cyclists have the comfort of competing in a couple of races throughout the year regardless of the intensity of the training. So each race must be kept with the proper remembrance and mementos. How exactly can you capture races and events on Evernote? Here are some ways this can be achieved:

- You ask a friend to document your races from the start up until the finish line. You can keep memories of it through photos or videos and event reports. If it is a huge event being covered by the media and all, you can ask a copy of the video shot by some media personnel or keep parts of articles that gives you a fond idea of the event.

- Images and videos can be closely recorded and saved on your Evernote account. With your notebook, you will be able to categorize each race you've done and all the information that goes along with it.

• Due to the rarity of the events, you might want to take photos of every part of your cycling journey for each event. From the preparation stage until the event day.

• It is perfectly normal for people to keep photographic memorabilia on Evernote. You can save your cycling number, your entry forms, the people you've been with, the sponsorships et cetera. Physically keeping these memories may be a bother, as you will have to store them physically. But by storing photos of them on Evernote, it will be easy for you to look back and recollect the races.

• You can also write notes on your personal bests on all the races and look back at your progress. Do you need a quick reminder? Go ahead and it's readily available. Several years later you can show your kids and grandkids all the successful events you've joined and you can forever cherish those moments with a click of a few buttons. Forget the attic space, Evernote is an entirely new approach that requires so little to remember so much.

9.) Creating An Event Or Race Calendar

Cycling, just like all the other sports, should not be practiced only days before the event. You need a gradual increase on your biking miles to make sure you have a slow and steady build up of your cycling routine. A slow and steady way of reaching your goal is what Evernote is supposed to do. It also reminds you what events you need to be ready for and the information that goes with it.

When registering for an event, you need to be able to have a note that encapsulates everything about the race. Every bit of information is a big deal. Although the race is far away, you might be preparing for it at the wrong way. Perhaps, you might have gotten the distance wrong and you prepared for a sprint rather than a long distance cycling race. A few kilometers is forgivable, but if you've prepared for a 3 kilometer race and signed up for a 42 kilometers, then you will struggling. Distance means everything because the technique and pacing is extremely important. You will also need to remember the dates and the type of race. Would it be related to a triathlon, would it be on mountainous terrains? Being extremely prepared for the meticulous details will surely get you in a good finishing position, if not beating your personal best.

Your calendar will then need to be organized based on the type of race. You will have to set reminders on your training information and all each day. This will make it easier for you to plan out the rest of your training period before the event. By doing this, you don't have to recall all your training information and think about what you've done in your previous trainings and what you need to do next time. It just makes it easier to be focused. You don't only have to have reminders of your training schedules; you can keep a close eye on your diet in relation to your personal and professional life. Your trainings must be suitable to your living condition without putting too much strain on your body and relationships.

10.) Recording Your Heart Rate Zones

Health is an important part of any sport and keeping a close track on your health requirements and limitations should be the number one priority. Especially to someone who has a long history of health problems, you would need to monitor it closely. If ever something bad happens, your access to your health information is at easy access on Evernote.

What you are advised to do before going on any cycling expedition is to have a health clearance from a doctor or general practitioner. The purpose of this is to make sure you are physical ready to embark in a physically strenuous activity. Some people have taken advantage of this in the past with some mishaps along the way. Having a cull body check up won't take too much time and effort, but just by doing this in preparation, you will be all set in the future.

Once you have the go signal to workout and train, make sure you save your power meter or heart rate numbers on a note on Evernote. This information is handy if you are working with a trainer so you can show them your history. Manipulating or changing the results will not benefit you at all. All it does is that it just makes everything more complicated than it already is. This isn't only for one particular health area on your body; this is applicable to other health concerns.

You should also keep track of it during your training rides. The great thing about Evernote is that you can have it stored on your smartphone during your ride making it more accessible to see. Plus, it can be useful for anything that comes your way. It is no harm to be prepared just in case something happens than to not be prepared and panic after. Having a recording of your past heart rate zones and your current ones can also determine whether your heart is getting worse, getting better or maintaining a good heart rate. This will enable you to fix your training routines that will keep you healthy as well as preparing yourself for the event.

11.) Document Your Workout

Your event preparation will be the longest and hardest obstacle before the race day. At this moment, strict rules on diet and technique must be followed to reach the maximum result. Evernote allows you to document your workout to the tee so you won't be forgetting things. Reminders are set up to keep you on track. But just a note, although Evernote provides all these features for the cyclist to embark on, you must be ready to invest your time and effort in it also.

• Keep your workout notes readily available. Your warm ups have to be noted and allocated on your workout schedule. Make sure that you are able to warm up completely that the muscles that you will be focusing on are properly stretched. You don't want any cramps in between your workout.

• During cycling, you have to vary your workouts on different sports. Although cycling only requires a bike, swimming and running is perfect to tone your body more to make it easier for you to bike.

• Reminders need to be put in place for you to have enough rest days. Evernote gets an overview of your workout schedule and you'll need to allocate enough time for you to rest. A strained body can only do so much on future trainings and the event. It's understandable that you want to do so much in order to be prepared, but you can't really reach your prime potential in a rush. A gradual build up is key.

• Don't forget to warm down! Through intense heat and muscle usage, you need to cool down to put yourself in the proper body temperature. This is put you from training mode, back to doing normal things. This would also help with muscle relief so you won't feel the stress of the workout later on. Remember that a warm down is as important as a warm up.

• Keep a journal on Evernote that documents everything that has happened in the work out. Whether you were exhausted with it, which parts of your body started aching, your heart rate levels. You will be able to track down your health progress as well as what you've done during the workout.

12.) Create A Race Packing List

Physical preparation has been discussed in the previous sections of this book, but equipment preparation is just as important. Imagine going through to race day forgetting your vital cycling gadgets. There have even been cases where people forgot their helmets, their cycling suit and even their bikes! Being fully prepared is the key to success and Evernote will remind you with what you need to have at the ready at all times.

A packing list is extremely important. During race day, you will be so excited and nervous that your head will be concentrated on finishing the race at a good time. You might be so busy that you forget your underwear, your cycling glasses or your lucky charm. A packing list can be divided into notes and saved as reminders. You can have a packing list right before the event before you head out or a packing list that you need to have a few days before. The packing list that you need a few days before usually consist of meals, snacks and other last minute equipment that you might need in the ready. You can't expect to buy bananas for protein months before the event that will be ridiculous. Usually, a checklist that you have on the day is just to make sure that your equipment is together. If you're prone to forgetting something important, check your list over and over again just to make sure. You can even send the list via Evernote email address to a friend who will be accompanying you to have a second person's opinion of your things just in case.

A packing list isn't the only thing that you should remind yourself to bring. You should have a reminder a few days before the event to actually check your gear. You'll have enough time by then to make sure that your tires aren't flat or if the screws on your seat are loose. The success of your instrument is the success of you. You can only do so much if when at the finish line you have a flat tire and you're moving at snail's pace. Therefore, packing and preparing your things through a checklist and planned schedule can mean a lot.

12.1) Create reminders for consumables

Whenever you replace something on your bike like a chain or cassette, create a note with a reminder to order a new one to replace it, may 3 months or 6 months from now depending on how many miles you ride.

Sports In General

13.) Managing Fantasy Sports Hobbies

Fantasy sports hobbies are games that allow people to create and manage their own teams based on real life players and their abilities. It just gives another dimension to a personalized dimension in sports that gives the imagination of controlling your squad based on personal taste. Some people take this hobby to great heights that organization and command of their teams are parallel to their organization and command on their work and personal life. How does it work?

- When it comes to draft picking your team, Evernote allows to have a thick research on who you should get on your squad taking to account their positions, weaknesses, injuries and real life drafts. Early preparation is advised so you will know exactly your list of players to have. You can access the web clipper function on Evernote to collect all the valuable information on certain payers. Through the season, you'll be able to refer to all the details in one area rather than have bookmarked websites to flick through.

    ☐ Environmental benefit: you won't have to print pages upon pages of research to keep yourself up to date. The best thing about it is to have it all in one place so as to not bother with physical storage.

- You can then add a tag to the notes you've created based on different categories and subcategories. You can have the option of storing them on their positions, their teams or their strings under the type of sport you are managing. You can even have different tags for the National Football League or your team on the Barclay's Premier League.

- You can use Skitch to take photos of the scores that your team has won. This isn't so much managing asset, rather the benefit is that you will then be able to show it off to your friends who have lost against you. A great perk to keep a "friendly" competition lively. Great emphasis on the friendly part.

• Due to Evernote's constant and useful reminders, you will be able to manage your team in a more efficient way. You will be able to refresh your memory on which players need to be traded next season as well as the overall notices on the performance of players and past trades.

14.) Winning In Fantasy Football

People managing fantasy football teams don't go through all the effort to play for fun. The fun usually comes after winning. There are plenty of people that solemnly promise that their fantasy football teams are for the entertainment and pleasure of the ability to manage your own squad. Lies. Although it may be fun in the beginning, there comes a point where your troubles must leave you to a win. You will need all the support you can get; therefore we have a few tips that Evernote can lead you to victory.

• There is no better way of managing something than have a reminder keeping you up to date on what you need to do. The whole purpose in fantasy football is organization and Evernote's reminder feature does just that. You'll need to decide on which players are on the starting string, which players are injured and when they'll be ready enough to start playing. Just by reminding yourself to decide on the roster, you will be ready for a anything the opponent can throw at you. Also your reminder can set up a deadline during trade season. You wouldn't want to eye a valuable player and miss the deadline by a couple of hours, that will hurt more than heartbreak, believe me.

• Evernote's web clipper allows you to browse through online sources for information regarding players you've placed on your watch list. By understanding each player and their capabilities in a place that is easily accessible and compared, you can easily snap up a trading deal and have your dream team set for the season.

• Finances in a club are vital. By keeping a checklist on the people that still needs to pay their dues and who needs to be paid out, you will be able to cover that aspect without the hassle.

• Although fantasy football is primarily organizing and improving your team, you can still share notes and have notes shared to you from other players. Evernote encourages this so you will be up to date with the current happenings. This is important when there are sudden changes and notices. Your readiness and adaptability to change is a great trait in winning.

15.) Dominate Your Fitness

Being fit and maintaining your fitness regiment is one of the greatest struggles we have to face daily. In theory, being fit is straightforward. All you have to do is to eat the right food and go through the proper exercise. False. It is a mixture of various other factors and temptations and fitness promises usually last no more than a few weeks, if not days without the right guidance. How will Evernote help you dominate your fitness?

• You will be able to store all your fitness information on all your devices with an Evernote application installed. This beats having one device that you have to bring wherever you go. You can track what you eat at work through your desktop and have your training figures on your smartphone when going on a run.

• Did I mention it is free? Having all these features in one device is a great thing and having to pay nothing for it is even better. Although the premium upgrade is ideal, starting off with Evernote and getting the hang of things are great when you pay zilch.

Here are the steps on what maintain your fitness:

1. You can take snaps of your workouts and store them on your Evernote account. This will collate what you need to do. Although you can track it on paper, you might lose them and stress is a mess for fitness people.

2. Tag your workouts according to the notebooks that they are associated with. It just makes it easier for you to find what you need. Have difficulty remembering your gym workouts on a Wednesday? Have no fear Evernote is here.

3. Did you know that Evernote could detect your handwriting? I know right, if you have legible handwriting, you can search words on

Evernote have it locate it for you. This is great in the cases where you've forgotten to tag them or added the wrong title.

4. If you're tired of typing and snapping, you can keep voice memos throughout your workouts. Perhaps, you can use it to remind yourself that you can bench press this many kilograms of weight and how many times you can do it for.

16.) Don't injure yourself, track your running shoes

If you're a runner I bet you track your weekly mileage. But do you track your running shoe's mileage? The vast majority of runners replace their shoes too late. Experts recommend replacing your shoes at most every six months and even better every 400 miles or so.

When you buy a new pair of shoes create a new note with a reminder 4 to 5 months in the future prompting you to order a new pair of shoes.

Conclusion

It is my hope that this book has given you a few new ideas on how to use of great app called 'Evernote'. It has discussed on topics such as how this application could simply be used with School as it could be used for your groceries. In constant pursuit to provide for you tips on what is best to do for each of the features created within Evernote for what situation.

Let's take a look back at one of the aspects that Evernote helps cater to: Technology. Technology in our modern times has provided us with constant access to worldwide knowledge, communication and advancements to make man survive the way they have for the past decade or so. But, with all these information, ideas and plans that we have for ourselves, how do we plan on keeping them when we need them? Imagine all the information we need to keep from personal documents, flight details or business meetings? With advancement in technology comes an overflow of information that is difficult to keep in one area. What this book likes to highlight, if it was not mentioned among the numerous chapters was that it is your personal digital archive. What people used to archive in the past are large sizes of vast amounts of notebooks that are kept in libraries. Now, it can all be kept within an application and that application is Evernote.

Being able to store all your information within one area, especially a digital area, leaves no paper trail resulting in reduced use of paper and reduced need to cut down trees. Making it eco-friendly for those nature lovers out there. Evernote can store everything from pictures, video, audio and links to everything you need to keep track of and information you need to know.

Whether you have simply skimmed through the book or thoroughly read through it, it should be obvious already that all the information you need to operate your Evernote application with productivity and ease is placed within the book. Where can you find a book that provides for you step-by-step instructions telling you how to work the application? That's what this book aims to please, to ensure that you know how to properly work all the features of this application to your advantage. Where can you find a book that provides more than just instructions? You may have encountered a book that just gives you tips or just gives you step-by-step instructions, but as you can see this provides both and more.

By allowing as much information to be placed within one book, information is easily accessible for you. What is even better is when you want to share this information with all your friends who have clutter filled and disorganized lives. Just introduce them to Evernote and show them this book to help improve their lives.

Don't be too shy to review this book again and again. You aren't expected to remember everything after the first try so be sure to keep this book for future needs. For example, you can review this books tip on how to use Evernote before you go on your next vacation trip. Be sure to read the chapter that discusses solely on how to use Evernote for travel. Another time you could use it is when your friend has requested advice from you on how to stay on track and be organized with their time. If you have reviewed the book, once you talk to them again they are going to look up to you and your advice. You may be improving their lives with the use of the tips given by this book.

It may take time to embrace the aspects and features of this application, but once you do it will definitely upgrade your life to the next level. This book has been proven to save you time? If it isn't apparent to you already, here's an example: If you wake up on a Sunday, which is the day you usually go grocery shopping but seeing as you have rushed to go to the store you have forgotten your list or have forgotten to create your list the night before. Now, having to go home again to see what it is you need you have now lost at least one or two hours of your time (depending on where you live) just because you have forgotten to write down your list. If you had placed it on Evernote the night before, you would have saved one or two hours out of your day to do something more productive like start on school work or catch up on your hobbies.

Being organized comes with the Evernote application. If you had read the book, it provides for you countless ways you can be organized with Evernote and without being organized, you will end up wasting your time and time is money. Organization applies to every aspect of our lives; being organized at home creates for a clutter-free environment, which in the end turns for a clutter-free life. The more organized your home is or your surroundings the better you will perform. This may also be in relation to having an organized surrounding during work. If you have organized your desk and your mind with the use of the note feature that Evernote has for you, then you will never end up missing a presentation or a meeting again. You are definitely in the right path to impressing your boss to a promotion.

All of these could be possible for you once you have embraced the idea of having a digital archive and not just any digital archive, the Evernote application digital archive. Embracing this new and modern application just goes to show that you are ready to embrace a more successful you.

So, be sure to keep this guide wherever you may be, master it and take advantage of it. You may not know it now, but this book and the Evernote application may be the key to your success for the future.